D0359588

IN THE DAYS
of THE
THE
ANGELS

STORIES & CAROLS FOR CHRISTMAS

WALTER WANGERIN, JR.
Author of *The Book of God*

WATERBROOK
PRESS

IN THE DAYS OF THE ANGELS
PUBLISHED BY WATERBROOK PRESS
2375 Telstar Drive, Suite 160
Colorado Springs, Colorado 80920
A division of Random House, Inc.

Scripture quotations are drawn from the author's own translation from the Greek as well as from *The Revised Standard Version of the Bible,* copyright © 1946, 1952, and 1971 by the Division of Christian Education of the National Council of the Churches of Christ in the USA. Used by permission.

"The Manger Is Empty," "The Hornbill," and "A Quiet Chamber Kept for Thee" originally appeared in *The Manger Is Empty: Stories in Time* by Walter Wangerin, Jr. (San Francisco: Harper-SanFrancisco, Zondervan), 1989.

ISBN 1-57856-395-X

Published in association with the literary agency of Alive Communications, Inc.,
7680 Goddard St., Suite 200, Colorado Springs, CO 80920

Library of Congress Cataloging-in-Publication Data
Wangerin, Walter.
    In the days of the angels : stories and carols for Christmas / Walter Wangerin, Jr.—1st ed.
        p.   cm.
    ISBN 1-57856-395-X
    1. Christmas—Literary collections.   I. Title

PS3573.A477 I5 2000
813'.54—dc21   00-043246

Printed in the United States of America
2000—First Edition

10 9 8 7 6 5 4 3 2 1

To Deborah
My sister in blood and in blessing

CONTENTS

THE MANGER
IS EMPTY

My daughter cried on Christmas Eve. What should I say to the heart of my daughter? How should I comfort her?

Her name is Mary. She's a child. She wasn't crying the tears of disillusionment, as adults do when they've lost the spirit of the season. And she trusts me. I do not lie. My Mary is easily able to throw her arms around me in the kitchen and to hang on with a hug—proving that she trusts me. Neither, then, was she weeping the tears of an oversold imagination that Christmas Eve. She hadn't dreamed a gift too beautiful to be real, nor had she expected my love to buy better than my purse.

Nor was she sick. Nor was she hungry for any physical thing.

No, Mary was longing for Odessa Williams, that old black lady. Mary was longing for her life. That's why she was crying.

Too suddenly the child had come to the limits of the universe. A casket. She stood at the edge of emptiness and had no other response than tears. She turned to me and wept against my breast, and I am her father. And should I be mute before such tears? What should I say to the heart of my daughter Mary?

We have a custom in our congregation: Always we gather on the Sunday evening before Christmas, bundled and hatted and happy, and we go, then, out into the sharp December darkness to sing carols. Down the streets of the city we go, the children bounding forward, adults all striding behind, chattering, making congenial noises, puffing ghosts of breath beneath the streetlights, laughing and glad for the company. Does anyone think it will snow? It's cold enough to snow, and the air is still, and the stars are already a snow-dust in heaven.

It's a common, communal custom. You do it too?

We crowd on the porches of the old folks. The children feel a squealing excitement because they think we're about to astonish Mrs. Moody in her parlor by our sudden appearing—carols from the out-of-doors, you know. She'll be so-o-o-o surprised! So they giggle and roar a marvelous *Hark!* with their faces pressed against her window: *Hark! The herald angels sing, Glory to the newborn king—*

Mrs. Moody turns on her porch light, then opens her curtains, and there she is, shaking her head and smiling, and the children fairly burst with glee. They can hardly stand it, to be so good. She turns on her porch light, and here we are, fifteen, maybe twenty of us, spilling down her steps into the little yard, lifting our faces, lifting our voices—doing silly things, like lifting our key-rings to the refrain of "Jingle Bells" and making a perfect, rhythmic jangle. Everybody's willing to be a kid. Nobody minds the cold tonight. The white faces among us are pinched with pink, the black ones (we are mostly black ones) with frost, as though the cold were a white dust on our cheeks.

And down the street we go again, and so we sing for Mrs. Lander and Mrs. Smith and Mrs. Buckman and Mrs. DeWitt.

And though we can be silly, and though this is just an ordinary custom, yet we are no ordinary choir. No: Many of us sing for "The Sounds of Grace," a choir of legitimate repute. And some of us have been blessed by God with voices the angels would weep to own.

For sometimes on that Sunday evening, by a decision that no one understands, Timmy Moore will begin a solo in a husky and generous tenor voice. *O holy night,* the young man starts to sing, and then we are all an audience, listening in a starry dark. *It is the night of the dear Savior's birth. Long lay the world,* sings Timmy Moore. We bow our heads. Mrs. DeWitt, on the inside of her window, bows her head. We are more than an audience. We are passengers. This strong voice is a sort of chariot, you know, able to carry us out of the streets of the city, through dark night, to the fields of shepherds far away. *Fall on your knees,* sings Timmy Moore, huge and strong, transported: *O hear the angel voices! O night divine! O night when Christ was born.* There is locomotive power in this, and truth, and utter conviction, and we can scarcely breathe. *O night! O night divine.*

4

So then, Timmy is silent. And what then? Why, then we all sing "Silent Night." And then occurs such a sweet and delicate wonder that Mrs. DeWitt looks up with the astonishment that the children had expected at first, but which none of the children notice now—for they are caught in the wonder too. Mrs. DeWitt looks up and starts to cry. She covers her mouth with an aged hand, and she cries.

For on the third verse of "Silent Night," Dee Dee Lawrence, that blinking child, soars high and high above us all on a descant so beautiful it can break your heart. Dee Dee simply flies, high and light, precise, to the stars themselves, to the crystal sphere of heaven, and we are singing too, but we have forgotten we sing. Dee Dee is the winter's bird, singing: *Son of God, love's pure light, Radiant beams from thy holy face*— And when that child has reached the crystal sphere, with the wing of her music she touches it, and all the round sky rings. The night is alive. This is the wonder that catches us all. *With the dawn of redeeming grace,* sings Dee Dee Lawrence, and then she sinks to the earth again: *Jesus, Lord, at thy birth,* descending, descending—innocent, I think, of the thing she has just accomplished—finding her place in the midst of earthly voices again. *Jesus, Lord, at thy birth.* And she is done. And we are done. We move in quietness to the next house.

Dee Dee Lawrence has a round, milk-chocolate face and an oriental cast to her eyes. Her beauty is not remarkable. Until she sings.

As we walk to the next house, we become aware that we, with Mrs. DeWitt, have been crying. That's why we are quiet. The tears are icy on our cheeks.

But these are good, contemplative tears. They are not like the tears my Mary cried on Christmas Eve.

And so it was that on Sunday evening, the twentieth of December 1981, we kept our custom and went out caroling. Mary was seven years old then. Dee Dee was eight. Timmy was with us, and the Hildreth children. Most of the children's choir, in fact, had come along. The night was not much different from those that went before—except for this, that when we had finished our round of houses we went to St. Mary's Hospital to sing for several members who were patients at Christmastime. We divided into three groups. As pastor, I myself led a handful of children to the room of Odessa Williams because her condition was worse than the others.

It was Odessa Williams who made the night different.

The children had never laid eyes on her before. When they crept into the ward and saw her cadaverous body, they were speechless for a while. Scared, I think. Mary's blue eyes grew very large, and I felt pity for her.

Well, I knew what to expect, but Mary didn't. I had been visiting the woman for several years now—first in her apartment, where she'd been housebound, then in the nursing home—and I had watched the wasting of Odessa.

Two years ago she had been a strapping tall woman of strong ways, strong opinions, and very strong affections. Fiercely she had loved the church that she couldn't actually attend. She'd kept abreast of congregational activities by telephone, by a gossip-system, by bulletins and newsletters and friends—and by me. She pumped me for information every time I visited her, puffing an endless chain of cigarettes, striding about her apartment in crushed slippers, waving her old black arms in strong declaration of the things she thought I ought to do and the things I ought not, as pastor, to be doing.

I had learned, for my own protection, to check her

mouth as soon as I entered her room. If the woman wore dentures, she was mad: She wanted her words to click with clarity, to snap and hiss with a precision equal to her anger. Mad at me, she needed teeth. But if she smiled a toothless smile on me, then I knew that her language would be soft and that I had her approval—that week. She was particularly fierce regarding her children, the choir, the "Sounds of Grace," though she had never heard them sing. She loved them. She swelled with a grand, maternal love for them. And if ever I had not, by her estimate, done right by these children, the teeth in the mouth of Odessa Williams were the flashing, clacking weapons of an avenging angel.

It will be understood why I was never able to persuade the woman to stop smoking. Even in the nursing home she continued to smoke. But the disease that kept her housebound and sent her to the nursing home was cancer.

Cancer, finally, had laid her in the hospital.

And it was cancer that frightened the children when they crept around her bed on Sunday night, come to sing carols to her. It put the odor of warm rot in the air. It had wasted Odessa to bone.

Mary and Dee Dee and Timmy and the others tried to touch nothing in the little space, not the bed, not the wall behind them. They grew solemn, unable to take their eyes from the form before them. One little lamp shed an orange light on the hollows of Odessa's face, sunken cheeks and sunken temples and deep, deep eyes. The lids of her eyes were thin as onion skin, half-closed; and her flesh was dry like parchment; and the body that once was strapping now resembled broomsticks in her bed—skinny arms on a caven stomach, fingers as long as chalk. And who could tell if the woman was breathing?

Mary stood across the bed from me, not looking at me, gazing down at Odessa. Mary's eyes kept growing larger.

So I whispered to all of them, "Sing." But they shuffled instead.

"What's this?" I whispered. "Did you lose your voices? Do you think she won't like it?"

"We think she won't hear," said Mary.

"No, no, sing the same as you always do," I said. "Sing for Miz Williams."

Well, and so they did, that wide-eyed ring of children, though it was a pitiful effort at first. "Away in the Manger," like nursery kids suspicious of their audience. But by the time the cattle were lowing, the children had found comfort in the sound of their own voices and began to relax. Moreover, Odessa had opened her eyes, and there was light in there, and she had begun to pick out their faces, and I saw that Mary was returning Odessa's look with a fleeting little smile. So then they harked it with herald angels, and they found in their bosoms a first noel that other angels did say, and then a marvelous thing began to happen: Odessa Williams was frowning—frowning and nodding, frowning with her eyes squeezed shut, frowning, you see, with fierce pleasure, as though she were chewing a delicious piece of meat. So then Mary and all the children were grinning, because they knew instinctively what the frown of an old black woman meant.

Odessa did not have her dentures in.

And the marvelous thing that had begun could only grow more marvelous still.

For I whispered, "Dee Dee," and the innocent child glanced at me, and I said, "Dee Dee, 'Silent Night.'"

Dear Dee Dee! That girl, as dark as the shadows around her, stroked the very air as though it were a chime of glass. (Dee Dee, I love you!) So high she soared on her crystal voice, so long she held the notes, that the rest of the children hummed and harmonized all unconsciously, and they began to sway together. *Round yon virgin, mother and child....*

Odessa's eyes flew open to see the thing that was happening around her. She looked, then she raised her long, long arms; and then lying on her back, the old woman began to direct the music. By strong strokes she lifted Dee Dee Lawrence. She pointed the way, and Dee Dee trusted her, so Dee Dee sang a soprano descant higher and braver than she had ever sung before. Impossible! Stroke for stroke with imperious arms, Odessa Williams gathered all her children and urged them to fly, and sent them on a celestial flight to glory, oh! These were not children anymore. These were the stars. Their voices ascended on fountains of light to become the very hosts of heaven—so high, so bright and holy and high. *Jesus, Lord, at thy birth!* So beautiful.

And then that woman brought them down again, by meek degrees to the earth again, and to this room and to her bedside; and there they stood, perfectly still, smiling in silence and waiting. How could anyone move after such a wonder?

Nor did Odessa disappoint them. For then she began, in a low and smoky voice, to preach.

"Oh, children—you my choir," Odessa whispered. "Oh, choir—you my children for sure. An' listen me," she whispered intently. She caught them one by one on the barb of her eye. "Ain' no one stand in front of you for goodness, no! You the bes', babies. You the absolute *best*."

The children gazed at her, and the children believed her completely: They were the best. And my Mary, too, believed what she was hearing, heart and soul.

"Listen me," Odessa said. "When you sing, wherever you go to sing, look down to the front row of the people who come to hear you sing. There's alluz an empty seat there. See it?" The children nodded. They saw it. "Know what that empty space is?" The children shook their heads. "It's me," she said, and they nodded. "It's me," she whispered in the deep orange light. "'Cause I alluz been with you, children. An' whenever you sing, I'm goin' to be with you still. An' you know how I can say such a mackulous thing?" They waited to know. She lowered her voice, and she told them. "Why, 'cause we in Jesus," she whispered the mystery. "Babies, babies, we be in the hand of Jesus, old ones, young ones, and us and you together. Jesus, he hold us in his hand, and ain' no one goin' to snatch us out. Jesus, he don' never let one of us go. Never. Not ever—"

So spoke Odessa, and then she fell silent. So said the woman with such conviction and such fierce love that the children rolled tears from their open eyes, and they were not ashamed. They reached over and patted the bones of her body beneath the blankets.

Mary's eyes, too, were glistening. The woman had won my daughter. In that incandescent moment, Mary had come to love Odessa Williams. She slipped her soft hand toward the bed and touched the tips of Odessa's fingers, and she smiled and cried at once. For this is the power of a wise love wisely expressed: to transfigure a heart, suddenly, forever.

But neither were these like the tears that Mary wept on Christmas Eve.

2.

On Tuesday, the twenty-second of December, Odessa Williams died.

It had been a long time coming, but was quick when it came. She died in her sleep and went to God without her dentures.

Quick when it came, I say: Odessa left us little time to

mourn for her. Gaines Funeral Home had less than a day to prepare her body, because the wake would take place on Wednesday evening. The funeral itself had to be scheduled for Thursday morning. There was no alternative. Friday was Christmas Day; Saturday and Sunday were the weekend; Gaines would be closed for three days straight; and Monday was too far away to make Odessa wait for burial. She would be buried, then, on Christmas Eve day.

And I, for my own part, was terribly distracted by a hectic week. This was the very crush of the season, you see, with a children's pageant and extra services to prepare. My pastoral duty was already doubled; Odessa's funeral tripled it. So I rushed from labor to labor, more pastor than father, more worker than wise.

Not brutally, but somewhat busily at lunch on Wednesday, I mentioned to my children that Miz Williams had died. They were eating soup. This was not an unusual piece of news in our household; our congregation had its share of elderly.

I scarcely noticed, then, that Mary stopped eating and stared at her bowl of soup.

I wiped my mouth and rose from the table.

"Dad?"

I was trying to remember what time the children should be at church to rehearse the Christmas program. Timing was everything. I wanted to give them a last instruction before I left.

"Dad?"

One thirty! "Listen—Mom will drive you to church at one fifteen. Can you all be ready then?"

"Dad?"

"Mary, what?" She was still staring at the soup, large eyes lost behind her hair.

"Is it going to snow tomorrow?" she said.

"What? I don't know. How would I know that?"

"It shouldn't snow," she said.

"You always wanted snow at Christmas."

In a tiny voice she whispered, "I want to go to the funeral."

Well, then that was it: She was considering what to wear against the weather. I said, "Fine," and left.

Thursday came grey and hard and cold and windless. It grudged the earth a little light and made no shadow. The sky was sullen, draining color from the grass and the naked trees. I walked to church in the morning.

We have a custom in our congregation: Always, before a funeral service begins, we set the casket immediately in front of the chancel and leave it open about an hour. People come for a final viewing of the body: friends who couldn't attend the wake, acquaintances on their way to work, strangers out of the past, memories, stories that will never be told. The dead one lies the same for all who gaze at her, infinitely patient. So people enter the church, and they creep up the aisle, and they look, and they think, and they leave again.

Soon some of the mourners remain. They keep their coats on, but they sit in the pews and wait. They remind me of winter birds on telephone wires, their plumage all puffed around them, their faces closed, contemplative.

And then, ten minutes before the service, I robe myself and stand in the back of the church to meet the greater flow of mourners. Last of all the family will arrive in limousines. I keep peeping out of the door to see whether the silent cars have slid to their places at the curb—

And so it was that on Christmas Eve at eleven in the morning I discovered Mary outside the door. In fact, she was standing on the sidewalk while her mother parked the car. She was staring at the sullen sky.

"Mary?" I said. "Are you coming in?"

She glanced at me. Then she whispered, "Dad?" as though the news were dreadful. "It's going to snow."

It looked very likely to snow. The air was still, the whole world bleak and waiting. I could have agreed with her.

"Dad?" she repeated more urgently, probing me with large eyes—but what was I supposed to do? "It's going to snow!" she said.

"Come in, Mary. We don't have time to talk. Come in."

She entered the church ahead of me and climbed the stairs in the narthex, then she started up the aisle toward the casket. She was seven years old. She was determined. Though robed and ready to preach, and though people sat face-forward on either side, I followed her.

Mary hesitated as she neared the chancel—but then took a final step and stopped.

She looked down into the casket. "Oh, no," she murmured, and I looked to see what she was seeing.

Odessa's eyes seemed closed with glue, her lips too pale, her color another shade than her own, a false, woody color. Her skin seemed pressed into its patience. And the bridge of her nose suffered a set of glasses. Had Odessa worn glasses? Yes, sometimes. But these were perched on her face a little askew, so that one became aware of them for the first time. Someone else had put them there. What belonged to the lady anymore, and what did not?

These were my speculations.

Mary had her own.

The child was reaching her hand toward the tips of Odessa's fingers, fingers like sticks of chalk; but she paused and didn't touch them. Suddenly she bent down and pressed her cheek to the fingers, then pulled back and stood erect.

"Dad!" she hissed. Mary turned and looked at me and did not blink but began to cry. "Dad!" she whispered, accusing. "It's going to snow, and Miz Williams is so cold." Immediately the tears were streaming down her face. "Dad!" she wept. "They can't put Miz Williams in the grave today. It's going to snow on her grave. It's going to snow on Miz Williams—"

All at once Mary stepped forward and buried her face in my robes. I felt the pressure of her forehead against my chest—and I was her father again, no pastor, and my own throat grew thick.

"Dad," sobbed Mary. "Dad, Dad it's Christmas *Eve!*"

These were the tears. These were the tears my daughter cried at Christmas. What do I say to these tears? It is death my Mary met. It's the end of things. It's the knowledge that things *have* an end, good things, kind and blessed things, things new and rare and precious, and their goodness doesn't save them; that love has an end; that people have an end; that Odessa Williams, that fierce old lady who seized the heart of my Mary and possessed it just four days ago, who was so real in dim light, waving her arms to the music of the children, that *she* has an end, has ended, is gone, is dead.

How do I comfort these tears? What do I say?

I said nothing.

I knelt down. I took my Mary's face between my hands but couldn't hold her gaze. I gathered her to myself and hugged her tightly, hugged her hard, hugged her until the sobbing passed from her body; and then I released her.

I watched her go back down the aisle like a poker soldier. She turned in a pew and sat with her mother. I saw that her lips were pinched into a terrible knot. No crying anymore. No questions anymore. Why should she ask questions when there were no answers given?

So: the funeral. And so: the sermon. And so I was the pastor again.

This was the text: "But there will be no gloom for her that was in anguish." The prophet Isaiah. It had seemed a perfect text, both for the season and for Odessa. "The people who walked in darkness have seen a great light," I read. That prophecy had come true in Jesus. It would become a truth again for the fierce old woman whose memorial this was. And for us too, since we were mourning now, but we would be celebrating tonight. I read: "For unto us a child is born, unto us a son is given—" *Christmas!* I said somewhere in my sermon. *Light is shining everywhere across the world, as light is shining first and perfectly in heaven! None who die in the Lord do die in darkness—*

But what were Isaiah and prophecy and all the sustaining truths of Christendom to my daughter Mary? She sat through the sermon with pinched lips and a sidelong stare. What was heaven to her? Nothing. Odessa had been something to her. You could touch and love Odessa. But Odessa was dead. The casket was closed. Death was something to her now, and maybe the only thing.

Later, at Oak Hill Cemetery, the people stood in greatcoats round the casket, shivering. My breath made ghosts in the air as I read of dust and ashes returning to dust and ashes. Mary said not a word nor held her mother's hand nor looked at me—except once.

When we turned from the grave, she hissed, "Dad!" Her blue eyes flashing, she pointed at the ground. Then she pointed at the sky. At the roots of the grasses was a fine, white powder; in heaven was a darker powder coming down. It was snowing.

3.

We have several customs—in our church and in my family—on Christmas Eve: As to the church, we celebrate the evening always with a children's pageant of the birth of Jesus. There never was the pageant in which my children didn't participate. As for my family, we always open our Christmas presents after the pageant is over, when the glow is still upon us, when Thanne and I can watch the children and enjoy their joy. Nothing is dearer to me than the purity of their gladness then, the undiscordant music of their laughter then.

And nothing could grieve me more, than that one of my children should be sad and lose the blessings of these customs.

Therefore, I worried terribly for Mary all Thursday through. As it happened, she was to be *the* Mary of the pageant, the Virgin, the mother of the infant Jesus. At three in the afternoon I left church and went home to talk with her.

I found her alone in her bedroom, lying on the bed and gazing out the window, her chin on her wrists. Snow clouds caused a darkness within, but she'd left the lights off where she was.

I stood beside the bed and touched her. The pragmatic pastor was concerned whether this child could accomplish so public a role in so private a mood. The father simply wished he knew what his daughter was thinking.

"Mary," I said, "do you want us to get another Mary?"

She kept watching the snow come down. Slowly she shook her head. "No," she said. "I'm Mary."

I didn't think she'd understood me—and if she didn't, then my question must have sounded monstrous to her ears. "For the pageant, I mean," I said, "tonight."

But she repeated without the slightest variation, "I'm Mary."

Mary, Mary, so much Mary—but I wish you weren't sad. I wish I had a word for you. Forgive me. It wasn't a kind world after all.

"You are Mary," I said. "I'll be with you tonight. It'll be all right."

We drove to the church. The snow lay a loose inch on the ground. It swirled in snow devils at the backs of the cars ahead of us. It held the grey light of the city near the earth, though this was now the night, and heaven was oblique in darkness. Surely the snow covered Odessa's grave as well, a silent, seamless sheet.

These, I suppose, were Mary's thoughts, that the snow was cold on the new-dug grave. But Mary's thoughts confused with mine.

The rooms of the church were filled with light and noise, transfigured utterly from the low, funereal whispers of the morning. Black folk laughed. Parents stood in knots of conversation. Children darted, making ready for their glad performance, each in a different stage of dress, some in blue jeans, some in the robes of the shepherds two

23

millennia and twenty lands away. Children were breathless and punchy. But Mary and I moved like spirits through this company, unnoticed and unnoticing. I was filled with her sorrow, while she seemed simply empty.

In time the wildness subsided. The actors huddled in their proper places. I sat with the congregation, two-thirds back on the right-hand side. The lights in the sanctuary dimmed to darkness. The chancel glowed a yellow illumination. The pageant began, and soon my daughter stood with pinched lips, central to it all.

"My soul," said Mary, both Marys before a little Elizabeth—but she spoke so softly that few could hear, and my own soul suffered for her: "My soul," she murmured, "magnifies the Lord, and my spirit rejoices in God my Savior—"

And so: The child was surviving. But she was not rejoicing.

Some angels came and giggled and sang and left.

A decree went out.

Another song was sung.

And then three figures moved into the floodlit chancel: Joseph and Mary—and one other child, a sort of innkeeper–stage manager who carried the manger, a wooden trough filled with old straw and a floppy doll in diapers.

The pageant proceeded, but I lost the greater part of it in watching my daughter.

For Mary stuck out her bottom lip and began to frown on the manger in front of her—to frown fiercely, not at all like the devout and beaming parent she was supposed to portray. At the *manger* she was staring, which stood precisely where Odessa's casket had sat that morning. She frowned so hard, blacking her eyes in such deep shadow, that I thought she would break into tears again, and my mind raced over things to do when she couldn't control herself any longer.

But Mary did not cry.

Instead, while the shepherds watched over their flocks by night, my Mary played a part that no one had written into the script. Slowly she slipped her hand into the manger and touched the doll in diapers. She lifted its arm on the tip of her pointed finger, then let it drop. *What are you thinking, Mary?* All at once, as though she'd made a sudden decision, she yanked the doll out by its toes, and stood up, and clumped down the chancel steps, the doll like a dishrag at her side. People made mild, maternal sounds in their throats. The rhythm of a certain angel faltered. *Mary, where are you going? What are you doing?* I folded my hands at my chin and yearned to hold her, hide her, protect her from anything, from folly and from sorrow. But she carried the doll to the darkened sacristy on the right and disappeared through its door. *Mary? Mary!*

In a moment the child emerged carrying nothing at all. Briskly she returned to the manger, up three steps as light as air, and down she knelt, and she gazed upon the empty straw with her palms together like the first Mary after all, full of adoration. And her face—Mary, my Mary, your face was radiant then!

O Mary, how I love you!

Not suddenly, but with a rambling, stumbling charge, there was in the chancel a multitude of the proudest heavenly host, praising God and shouting, "Glory to God in the highest!" But Mary knelt unmoved among them, and her seven-year-old face was smiling, and there was the flash of tears upon her cheeks, but they were not unhappy, and the manger, open, empty, seemed the receiver of them.

"Silent night, holy night—" All of the children were singing. "All is calm, all is bright—" The deeper truck-rumble of older voices joined them. "Round yon virgin mother and child—" The whole congregation was singing. Candlelight was passing hand to hand. A living glow spread everywhere throughout the church. And then the shock of recognition, and the soft flight followed: Dee Dee Lawrence allowed her descant voice its high, celestial freedom, and she flew. "Holy infant, so tender and mild—" *Mary, what do you see? What do you know that your father could not tell you? Mary, mother of the infant Jesus, teach me too.*

"Sleep in heavenly peace—" Having touched the crystal heaven, Dee Dee descended. The congregation sighed. Everybody sang: "Sleep in heavenly peace."

Mary sat immediately beside me in the car as we drove home. A sifting snow made cones below the streetlights. It blew lightly across the windshield and closed us in a cotton privacy. I had been driving in silence.

Mary said, "Dad?"

I said, "What?"

She said, "Dad, Jesus wasn't in the manger. That wasn't Jesus. That was a doll." *Ah, Mary, so you have the eyes of a realist now? And there is no pretending anymore? It was a doll indeed. So death reveals realities—*

"Dad?"

"What?"

She said, "Jesus—he doesn't *have* to be in the manger, does he? He goes back and forth, doesn't he? I mean, he came from heaven, and he was borned right here, but then he went back to heaven again, and because he came and went, he's coming and going *all* the time—right?"

"Right," I whispered. *Teach me, child. It is so good to hear you talk again.*

"The manger is empty," Mary said. And then she said more gravely, "Dad, Miz Williams' box is empty too. I figured it out. We don't have to worry about the snow." She stared out the windshield a moment, then whispered the next thing as softly as if she were peeping at presents: "It's only a doll in her box. It's like a big doll, Dad, and we put it away today. I figured it out. If Jesus can cross, if Jesus can go across, then Miz Williams, she crossed the same way too, with Jesus—"

Jesus, he don' never let one of us go. Never.

"Dad?" said Mary, who could ponder so much in her heart. "Why are you crying?"

Babies, babies, we be in the hand of Jesus, old ones, young ones, us and you together. Jesus, he hold us in his hand, and ain' no one goin' to snatch us out. Jesus, he don' never let one of us go. Never. Not ever—

"Because I have nothing else to say," I said to her. "I haven't had the words for some time now."

"Dad?"

"What?"

"Don't cry. I can talk for both of us."

It always was; it always will be; it was in the fullness of time when the Christ child first was born; it was in 1981 when my daughter taught me the times and the crossing of times on Christmas Eve; it is in every celebration of Christ's own crossing; and it shall be forever—that this is the power of a wise love wisely expressed: to transfigure the heart, suddenly, forever.

THE CAROL OF
WARM AND COLD

Mary, she blows on her knuckle
> *The wind so cold*
> *The night and the snow:*
Mary, she blows on her knuckle-bone;
Joseph, he blows on the coal.

The donkey that bore the young mother
> *Sing lullabies*
> *On perilous ice:*
The donkey that bore the young mother bore
The bearer of Jesus, our Christ.

Mary, she hasn't the ticking
> *Cold stone the floor*
> *And windy the door:*
Mary, she hasn't a mattress for
Catching her Christ and our Lord.

Joseph, he doffs his warm clothing
> *Binding the hay*
> *A cradle creating:*
Joseph, he makes of his woolen robe
Swaddling sheets for the babe.

We are the watchers who watch them
> *Two cries in the night,*
> *One pain, one delight:*
We are the watchers when Mary breathes
Breath in the infant and life.

We are the beasts and the singers
> *Ba! Ba!*
> *Gloria!*
We are the hosts and the herders who
See and remember the sight—

While Mary: she blows on her baby
> *The wind so cold*
> *The night and the snow:*
Mary, she kisses her baby's toes.
And Joseph, he brightens the coal.

THE HORNBILL

In the rain forests of Africa there lives a common, awkward bird. An ugly thing. Unbeautiful.

Nevertheless, I will honor her as a creature most exquisite, since she is the cursive script of our Creator. When she flies, her flight is the handwriting of God. When she nests, God is imparting parables.

This bird inhabits the cathedral darkness below high canopies of leaves. The vaulted space is green. Her world is loud with the shrieks of animals and dangerous with predators: jackals on the ground, the egg-eating bush babies in the branches, monkeys and serpents and, wheeling over all, the eagle. Carnivores. She lives in a perilous place. But she lives. She flies. Swift on her wing, she eludes her enemies and feeds on the fruit of the climbing vines, the high and flowering trees. She flies. At all times it is her nature and her freedom to fly—except when she mothers her children.

She's called the "hornbill" because she's got a beak as big as a hollow log, and on top of that beak, a horn. In every sense it's a megaphone beak, magnifying her cries and covering the whole of her face. The beak is a cannon in front of her, a peninsula, and affixed to the crest of it is a casque, a helmet, an enormous horn.

The hornbill's a large and ugly bird.

No! But she is terribly, terribly lovely.

Watch her. Watch what she does. Watch what she does to herself for the sake of her children.

For when the time draws nigh that she should lay and love a clutch of eggs, this ugly bird transfigures herself by sacrifice. She soars through the forest in search of the tree that has a hollow trunk to receive herself, her beak, and her eggs. When she has found it, she enters and flies no more.

Immediately, with the help of her mate from the outside, she sets to work to wall the doorway shut. Mud and dung make a hard cement: No predator will break in to terrorize the small chicks or to eat them. They are protected by her providence. Out of her bowels comes the stuff of their fortress wall. She is their refuge while they are weak. She is their space awhile.

But the wall that saves her children imprisons her!

There is no alternative: For the sake of her babies, she has exchanged the spacious air of the forest for a tight, dark cell and a crimped imprisonment.

And what does this mean? It means that a mother has sacrificed her freedom, which is to fly.

It means that she has sacrificed her independence, too. She is reduced to trusting absolutely in her mate.

Look: There is a slot in the wall she's constructed, a vertical gap exactly the shape of her beak. If the hornbill is to survive, she has to eat. If she's going to eat, her mate must bring the food—and then she will feed with peculiar intimacy, beak-to-beak through this slot, almost as if she were an infant herself. But for the love of her children, a mother accepts the loss and reduction.

Watch her. Watch that slot in the wall of dung. Food goes in, but things come flying out as well. The hornbill is fastidious. She twists in her prison, aims backward, and shoots her waste to the world outside with a stinging accuracy. In this way she keeps the nest immaculate. Moreover, she can burn the eye of a bush baby peeping in. She can change the mind of a monkey who thought to snatch a meal.

But watch her: For when the chicks are hatched and

tender, their mother fires one thing more from the slot—and this is the act that makes her so desperately lovely.

Feathers! One by one, her feathers fly out of the slot. But these are not the down of her breast; they are the longest, strongest feathers she has, the feathers by which she flies! In the small space of her nest, the shafts of these feathers would scratch and trouble her children; therefore, in extremist mercy, she strips her wings of their primary pinions, their primary purpose. And she strips herself of flight!

And what does this mean? That a mother has sacrificed her very nature for the sake and the saving of her children.

Thus is the hornbill exquisite.

She has become the very parable of love.

Jesus fulfilled what was spoken by the prophet, saying, "I will open my mouth in parables."

Who is the hornbill? Whom does she signify?

Read her, as once the ancient Christians read the whole book of nature—the mind of God made visible—then tell me, Christian: Who is she?

Well, who was it chose to leave the infinite sphere of heaven, willingly, compelled by loving alone?

Who denied himself celestial flight for the sake of a people? Who walled himself inside this narrow world, in time and in space, in a little frame of flesh, that he might be a refuge for the weary?

Who diminished himself to dependency—to a perfect, prayerful, infant dependency upon another—for the salvation of a people who thought themselves so marvelously independent?

Who plucked himself of power? Who sheared himself of his most glorious might, his blinding radiance, lest it harm us when we drew near to him? Who emptied himself and became an infant, swaddled in humanity, cradled in wood, flightless, bound to die?

Who loved us that much? Who loved us so purely, by such a sacrifice?

Of course. We are reading Christmas in an awkward bird.

O Jesus, born in our dark, reduced existence! O Savior, gentle in flesh beside me, you are the hornbill! And though the cross is vile, an engine of outrageous ugliness, you are not. You are beautiful.

I love you Lord Christ, and I want to fly.

O let me soar to brightness again. On your wing, oh!— carry me back to your heavens, and I will be free forever.

IN THE DAYS
OF THE ANGELS

i

In the days of the angels—
The hair on the necks of the people,
Didn't it stand like static?

In the days of the angels—
The air at their ears, the cloud in the heavens,
Didn't it crack like a solid?

In the days when the angels dropped,
Discharging news in the troposphere—
Could such electric language not
Have shot the nerves of the firmament
With signs? Signs?
White words and understanding?

Skin,
The abdomen,
And deep the human womb,
Must have been
Tympanic then.

Ho! In the days when archangels spoke—
Wasn't the scent of the weather ozone?
Tasting of seltzer and ions?
    And the look of the air thereafter—
Wasn't it crystalline, cleaner,
Dimensioned by nitrogen oxides,
Even as somebody's breathing
Swells with well-being?
Wasn't the breeze of the evening green?

    Surely the people perceived
That angels were immanent, speaking:

"*A son—*"
Now there's a bolt to strike an old man dumb.
One hundred bidders in the courtyard,
Jews devout at the hour of incense,
Should have been shocked in their nostrils,
Charged by a nitrogous excitement,
Their blood a rush of bubbles.

"*A Son—*"
Let a maiden grab her skirts and run.
Let citizens stare after her,
Stunned, wondering
Why Modesty goes forking through the streets,
Her knees indecently aflame,
Her hair unpinned, a fume on the wind:
"Cousin! Cousin, I've such a thing to tell you!"

"A virgin's Son—"
And the father who had not engendered it
Sprang from his pillow,
The crack of prophecy still ringing in his ears.
Surely Nazareth was startled with the man,
Surely Galilee!
Surely Rome
At such an impossible pop of lightning
Moaned in her sleep.

"A Savior!"
Then all the stars, the wheeling galaxy, streamed down
Exploding songs of fire across the firmament,
Sheeting the fields of shepherds in a flaming rain,
Gloria, roaring: *Gloria in altissimis Deo*,
The storm of heaven striking earth,
All angels in a fusillade!
Could anyone, could anyone have stayed asleep
When the whole air burned electric blue
And every hair on every head was singed?

Well,
If they did
They smelled the smoke in the morning
And did not understand
It was themselves
Whom God had
Scorched.

But the leaves grew greener in their season.
The vines were nourished by the nitrogen.
Oh, grapevines comprehend an angel's discharge—
And vineyards that year produced a wine so red
That fools who lifted glasses to the sun
Were made uneasy by the crimson lens
And the dim suspicion
They were drinking blood.

ii

But the salmon
    Shooting from a shattered water
    Knows;

And the falcon
    On her shelf of wind
    In the blink before she stoops;

And the doe who suddenly
    Lifts her face from a bank of fern
    Twisting her ears like dishes,

And the prairie dogs
    All standing watch on the tableland
    Erect as pepper shakers,

And the ant
    Twiddling her feelers in the universe,

And the rabbit
    Caught in the gloaming of the cougar,

And the krill
    Upheaving on the advent of oceanwater
    That precedes the grey whale—

All, all of these,
    At the terminal nerves of their beings,
    Know *Kairos,*
    The fullness of time:
    That the storm of the Lord is at hand.

They long for the crack of liberty
    Of all creation,
    Groaning an intensity
    Of waitfulness.

They have unsullied senses:
    Watch them. Call them kin.

Oh, ye nations!
    Let these be your angels!

MORAVIA

I.

Mother said that Aunt Moravia had grown steadily worse since coming to live with the family shortly after Paul was born. She said that in the beginning, Aunt Moravia was not so much crazy as creative and "exciting to have around," but that now she'd gone plain dotty.

Mother didn't make these observations with affection or a needling humor. It was, I think, her weariness speaking, so I disagreed with her. I thought Aunt Moravia had always been insane. Harmless, really, but vexing for those who had proper schedules and reasonable goals and normal views of existence.

As long as I knew her, Aunt Moravia was convinced that she had swallowed a glass piano. It caused, she said, a delicate and irritating music in her pancreas.

Near the end of dinner she would suddenly rise, place

one bony hand on her abdomen, the other on the small of her back, and whisper, "Do you hear it? *Liebling, Liebling,* can't you hear it?" Then, silently, she would begin to weep, would turn and retire to her bedroom.

"Liebling" was what she called my father, her nephew. Moravia was my great-aunt, actually. She was as old as stone.

When guests were scheduled she would grow restless and snappish. Just before they arrived, Aunt Moravia secluded herself in her bedroom. But as soon as conversation swelled to happy noises, shouts, laughter, the thin, bent woman would throw open her door and cry, "BAH, BA-BA-BA, BAH-DAH!" in a tremendous, yowling vibrato. It was "Pomp and Circumstance." She would sing "Pomp and Circumstance," the brass and the drums both, with an angry gusto straight through from beginning to end, then she'd slam the door. It took the bloom off the party rose.

I said, "Aunt Moravia, when people come to visit us, why do you sing?"

She opened her eyes wider and wider. She had no eyebrows or eyelashes any more. She said she lost them in the war. Instead, she wore fierce lines of black eye liner on her upper and lower eyelids, making me think of death or of God. And she had yellow teeth as long as pickets for fences.

"It is for shame upon your mother's meat," she hissed through these teeth.

I think Aunt Moravia liked me. She never pointed at me the way she pointed at my mother. Sometimes she would stand in the kitchen and raise her whole arm and point at mother for a full fifteen minutes, aiming her ragged fingernail wherever mother went as she cooked. Mom bowed her head and went about her business, very grim.

And Moravia answered my questions.

"What's the matter with my mother's meat?"

The old woman glared down her nose at me, though I was already a good head taller than she.

"Dressed to kill!" she declared. It came as divine judgment: "*Kein Demut!* No meekness in her roasts and gewgaws. Phaw! A haughty spirit before a fall!"

Mostly my Aunt Moravia wore black.

And then when I was seventeen, she began a new practice, neither crazier nor saner than anything else she did, yet very disturbing for me. Unreasonably, it always caused me to cry.

Aunt Moravia would emerge from her bedroom wild haired, naked under a silken nightgown, carrying high a burning candle. Her eyes without liner, the woman looked old and lost and defenseless. At first she'd stand baffled in the hallway, ten minutes, maybe twenty, but then she'd shuffle here and there for an hour or more, peering in every dark cranny of the house, and weeping: weeping.

No one knew of these midnight peerings—no one except myself. For in my seventeenth year I, too, initiated a private personal practice. After Mom and Dad and Debbie were sleeping, I regularly rose to work on certain drawings in a large, linen sketchbook. I did this in the tiny space of my closet, a cubbyhole for me—I mean, the hole of a cub that needs protection. But I could hear my Aunt Moravia, her uncertain tread, her soft weeping.

At first I thought she was looking for jewelry, because she had the habit of hiding her most expensive pieces (and Mom's as well) in odd, unfindable places. For example, she hid a single earring in a knothole in a basement joist. But she wasn't looking for jewelry.

During the late autumn of my senior year in high school, Aunt Moravia began to conclude her sad excursions by standing in the doorway of my closet, holding the candle aloft behind me in order to peer at my sketches.

The first time she did this, she dripped tears on my neck and shoulders. I thought it was hot wax, so I jumped and stifled a scream. Aunt Moravia's eyes went wide. She gasped and burst into something like infant tears, so I put my arms around her, and we held each other until neither one of us was sobbing anymore.

It was her weeping mostly. After that, the sound of her weeping while she searched through the house is what caused me to cry while I sketched.

Once I pointed at the pencil sketch of two hands rising to catch a football—just the hands, disembodied; I was trying to get them right—and I whispered, "Aunt Moravia, when you look at this, what do you see?"

"Nothing, Wilhelmus, sad to say. No, nothing at all."

"But then, what are you looking for?" I asked.

She shook her own head. Without the eyeliner, without lashes or eyebrows, her white hair and long face retained no severity at all. Age and a stunned sort of sorrow only.

She retreated. Carrying her candle backward through

the door frame of my closet, she said, "Wilhelmus, Wilhelmus, I am looking for the Son of God."

2.

I am a writer now. In fact, I was already planning to be a writer in the eighth grade, because awake I poured forth stories as easily as, asleep, I dreamed them.

In those days my sister Debbie listened to my stories. She's seven years younger than I am. She loved absolutely everything I said. But even Paul, four years older, would laugh and get lost in a good one. Paul—whom *I* loved and whom I venerated because he was handsome and virtuous and an athlete of outrageous aptitude—Paul became the hero, literally, of many a tale I told. During his own high-school years he was not ashamed to take me camping with him. In the buzzing darkness of the tent at night, I told him stories of his own tremendous feats, modeling the fiction on facts I myself had witnessed. Paul's personal grace was not to believe himself the hero, but rather to see my major character as a discrete and independent person, something that stood on its own. Really, there couldn't have been for me a higher praise or a better instruction than this, because what began as a homage became genuine art, a story living wholly by its own merits! I learned the craft of taking and making new. And best of all was that Paul invited me to camp with him *and his friends!* And guess what he asked me to do when we all were sitting round the fire? Yes. Tell a story.

They were seniors in high school, preparing to graduate and go off to college. I was a shock-headed kid in the eighth grade. Yet I described athletic action with such precision and such passion that they would shout and applaud. But it wasn't really for me. No, and that was the wonder: They were applauding the event they had just witnessed by means of me, my licorice mouth!

Well, and I never had the talent to be a jock. What I had was the admiration of the unable for the able—and by writing it, I lived it; I knew in the craft what my brother lived in the flesh. Oh, how I loved the high tension of personal challenge. I marveled at the strength and languor of long muscles stretching and clenching in a leopard's rhythm. I saw and I fixed in my memory the stunning beauty produced when extreme stress twists the torso and the pelvis against each other. And when I wrote the stories down, I delighted to describe contestants in the instant of peak accomplishment, out-doing themselves and *knowing* it, though all their attention was on the game, the achievement of an immediate goal.

That's Paul the football player, my model and my brother. How lithe and lovely and fierce his body in the dash and the lunge for a short pass, yes! But how serene his mind at the very same time! He made decisions and adjustments in the milliseconds of mid-flight.

I loved Paul. And I loved to tell stories. And after Paul had gone to college, Debbie got better and better at listening, so I got better and better at creating. And I was going to be a writer for sure. And I am a writer today. But there was that one year, my seventeenth year, when I neither wrote nor told a single tale; no one would have listened anyway; none of us cared, neither the teller nor the told.

So I took up the silent craft. I sketched. I sketched, and I wept. I drew things over and over again, until I got them right. Then I quit.

3.

On the Thanksgiving weekend of my junior year, Paul— himself a junior and a wide receiver for the university team—flew downfield with dazzling speed. Oh, how we all hooted and bellowed then! He planted his right foot, executed a quick buttonhook left, leaped like a salmon for a very high pass, and was struck from his right side at the knees.

We were watching the game on television. All of us. It was a ritual. Shouts and terrors and hilarity, my father's great waving of arms, my mother's more silent pride, Debbie's pink-faced passions, my laughter. And Aunt Moravia was singing tremendous stanzas of the German hymn, *Vom Himmel hoch, da komm' ich her!* Well, it's a Christmas song, and Christmas was coming; but I wouldn't swear it was because of Christmas that Moravia uttered this sacred descent of angelic choirs.

My brother's record was simply outstanding. There was serious anticipation that he would, within two weeks, receive the Heisman Trophy both for the quality of his game and for the pleasure of his person. This, though he was still a junior.

Yes: As good as his game was his goodness itself. Paul maintained humility even to Aunt Moravia's satisfaction, yet he looked people directly in their eyes and never blanched at their more rabid displays of possessiveness. If

Moses was, as Scripture says, "the meekest of men," then meekness means obedience to—and *only* to—the highest authority. Such obedience renders one both selfless and almighty bold, for the source of his behavior transcends the world's mutable rules and unstable affections. One who is accountable to God alone, yet peaceable on earth—that one is charismatic, whether others know the source and the reason or not. Paul had such a charisma. He genuinely loved God. My father would shout, "And don't we all?" Yes, of course we all loved God—but not as Paul did. My brother's athletic accomplishments were made heroic not because he was himself a demigod, but rather because he worshipped the one God and Creator of everything, even of his, Paul's, body. Obedience unto the Mind that made everything is what made Paul heroic.

In fact, I was fashioning these very concepts into a tale entitled "The Heisman Conundrum" when we saw Paul take that hit from the side. Helmet and shoulder pads, driving dead level with the ground, sent Paul's entire body up in a slow spin. He held the ball. He did not drop that criminal ball. While his legs ascended and his head clocked downward, he tucked the ball in the crook of one arm and crossed it with the other. So what? So there were no hands free to soften the fall. So when his pendulum head swept sideways over the ground there were no other bones to take the bloody weight of his body but the neck.

Mother groaned.

That was the only sound in our living room.

We sat still, watching for a space of time the huddle of managers and physicians. Watching nothing, actually, since Paul was hidden within them. When an ambulance drove out onto the field—not the flat-bed cart, not a stretcher borne between paramedics—Father said, "Neck's broke," and got up and left the room. I heard him dial the phone in the kitchen. Then he went outside.

Mom went into the kitchen and began to wash dishes.

Moravia placed her right hand on her abdomen, her left hand on the small of her back, and whispered, "Do you hear it? Wilhelmus, can't you *hear* it?"

But neither Debbie nor I were moving. Our eyes were glued to the set where a football game played in blue-grey flashes. We were waiting for some announcement, I think.

The phone rang in the kitchen. The back door banged open. Father said, "No, it's mine. Let me take it."

There was a pure black silence for a while, then I heard him cradle the receiver.

In a sort of dog-bark he said to my mother, "Con-firmed. Neck's broke." And again, he stalked outside.

4.

It was not my father's decision. It was my mother's quiet, uncompromising conviction that the whole family should fly to the city where Paul lay restrained in the intensive care ward of a very large hospital.

"Whole family" did not, however, include Moravia. Mother thought she ought to remain home.

But *"Liebling, Liebling,"* Moravia said to her nephew, my father, begging passage; and he, with a single snap of his head, granted her permission.

"If I'm paying, I'm choosing," he said.

Moravia came along.

The times when we were allowed to visit Paul in his unit were brief and restricted.

He had tubes in his nose, a maze of apparatus around his head and shoulders. His arms were tied down! Well, as I understood it, he had the capacity to move somewhat. But he would flex the wrong muscles at the wrong times and endanger himself—yet he refused to breathe hard on account of the unspeakable pain, and this was something he *should* do.

He looked caged. It scared me to see my brother so immobilized. Worst of all, he never recognized me. Never.

He recognized Mother. Not Father. He would talk to her, though it sounded more like whining. Oh, my brother Paul! In his big man's voice he made the noises of a spoiled child, beseeching Mom to "send him in" and crying because he wasn't being sent in. He said the coach was benching him for no good reason. He demanded that Mom go to the coach "right now, right *now*, and tell him that I'm quitting the team unless I get to play."

I went out of the unit and out of the hospital. I went to a movie alone.

After two days Dad, his lips pinched white, flew home. He said he had to work. He took Debbie with him, but not Moravia. I was left with Mom as a sort of support. I have no idea why Aunt Moravia stayed behind, too.

Then the doctor told us that Paul was developing pneumonia because he was making no effort to clear his lungs. He should cough. The doctor gave mom a plastic device in which four blue balls in four clear tubes would float upward on a cushion of air when the patient blew forcefully into its mouthpiece.

"Please," the doctor said, "persuade your son to blow the balls as high as he can."

Mom tried.

She sat in a chair by Paul's high bed and asked him to cough. "Just cough," she said.

He wouldn't.

In his whining voice, he said, "Hurts." He had a raggedy beard by now. His face was paste white and hollow.

"No, Paul, you *have* to," Mom said, "or the fluid in your lungs will kill you. Not your broken neck. And you can do something about fluid. Cough."

"Hurts, hurts," he said, shutting his eyes tight.

Mom stood and brought the plastic device to Paul's mouth. "Blow," she said. "Blow into this."

He didn't look. He didn't answer.

Mom said, "Make it a game, Paul. You're good at games. See how high you can make the blue balls go."

He glanced once at the device, then closed his mouth and curled the lips inward, between his teeth.

Mom pressed the mouthpiece into the line of his lips, saying, "Blow, Paul. You've *got* to blow."

He refused.

Mom pushed the mouthpiece harder. "Blow! Blow!" she said.

But Paul tightened the neck muscles. He seemed to want to turn his head.

"You can't do that!" Mom cried. "Do you *want* to die?" Paul opened his lips and said, "Dim you, dim you."

Immediately Mom grabbed his chin in her left hand, drove her fingers into his cheeks to force his jaws apart, then stuck the mouthpiece between his teeth.

But Paul bit down hard, pinching her fingers and snapping the plastic.

Mom slapped him.

"Cough!" she shrieked. "Cough, Paul! Cough! Cough!"

He didn't react at all. He lay inert with his eyes closed. There were tears at the lashes.

Mom lowered her face to his. She broke into terrible sobs. "I'm sorry, I'm sorry, I'm sorry," she said. "Oh, Paul, I am so sorry."

Dad visited on the weekends.

He never took Moravia home with him. When Mom asked, he didn't so much as answer her.

He did, however, bring Debbie to us when she got out of school for the holidays. It was his will that we should be an unbroken family on Christmas Day.

But Paul died on the morning of December twenty-four, the day before Christmas.

I have never doubted that Moravia knew first, before any of us, that Paul had ceased to breathe, for she began with absolutely no preliminary motion to sing softly, softly in German, *O Traurigkeit, O Herzeleid!* Truly, we had not expected that to be Paul's death day. Nor were we really convinced that he would die at all. Therefore her singing was at first an annoyance to my parents. But I knew. I looked at Moravia's wide, white eyes, their lids outlined in death black, the teeth as long and yellow as rodents' teeth, and I knew.

A nurse stepped into the unit, her eyebrows poised to criticize, but my little sister smiled up at her.

"It's okay," Debbie said, placating starched authority. "Aunt Moravia's crazy."

5.

There was, of course, no Christmas the year my brother died. Debbie longed for the ritual and felt sad for the lack. She told me so, after the season had passed from nothing into nothing. For her, our Christmas celebrations were like the bowl that held her liquid happiness, giving it place and a shape. She said she couldn't be sure she was happy if she didn't know where to find it.

But for the rest of us, Christmas died when Paul did. And happiness? The topic never came up.

It seemed to me that Dad tripled the time he spent traveling for his business. Through the winter and the spring and the summer he came home for...for what?— two weekends each month? Mom seemed to know which ones. We didn't. When autumn and football returned in the following year, my father watched no TV at all. It was like a divine proscription. *Thou shalt not...* whatever. And though he never said it aloud (he scarcely said anything aloud anymore) his glacial manner implied that I was violating the holy code each time I *did* watch a football game on television.

So it went. My mother began to wear sweaters. Heavy, shapeless, button-up sweaters. Against the cold, I supposed—except that she continued to wear them even in warm weather.

When I came into the kitchen after school, my tender mother would always stop cooking. She would wipe her hands on the apron that covered the sweater, then come to me and press her right palm to my forehead. "Oh, my dear, how *was* the day?" she'd say, and I would strive to answer. But a long lock of hair kept falling over her left eye, and though it had to obstruct her vision, she wouldn't notice. She wouldn't sweep it back again. That lock consumed my attention as surely as a ringing bell. The longer she let it hang, the less I could think of the news of my day, so I walked out of the kitchen, having said nothing at all.

A bit of a shambles was my mother. It occurred to me that this would be the perfect time to discuss the difference between craziness and creativity. A year ago I could have pulled it off with gentle humor, lifting my mother back into the smiling sunshine. But this year I couldn't muster the humor. Her sweaters and her hair and her docile ability to sense and to serve my father—these things disturbed me too much. I could put them out of my mind only when I put my mother out of my sight.

So it went. I stopped writing and started sketching. Body parts. Hands in a hundred figurations; legs running, leaping, squatting, flying; torsos in tension. I wanted to get them right. Arms, elbows, ankles, feet. The neck atwist.

One Saturday morning in May, Debbie rapped on my bedroom door and came in and saw the sketchbook open in my closet. I rushed to close it. I closed the closet door, too, and threw myself on the bed.

"What do you want, Deb?" I said.

She said, "Will you take me camping this summer?"

"Camping?"

"Paulie took you."

"When Paul took me," I said, "I was thirteen, not ten years old."

"It doesn't matter," Debbie said. "How old I am doesn't matter. I know that, Will, on account of last Thanksgiving Paulie told me he would take me camping the same as he took you, and I said, 'When?' and he said, 'Next summer.'"

My sister has a dark, narrow face. Her eyes can be intense without looking. They remind me more of mine than of Paul's, because Paul was gregarious, generous, social, open to absolutely anyone, never in need of privacy, a man of contentments. Debbie can be as private as I am. She's a reader. But she also knows how to share her privacy. She makes it a sort of gift to a small, enduring circle of friends.

"He promised 'Next summer,' Will," she said. "That's *this* summer. And the only age that matters is yours. You're seventeen. That's old enough. Please? Willie? Won't you take me camping?"

"Maybe."

Debbie stood looking at me for a while with no expression on her face. Her hair was very neat. She pulled it back so tightly that it shined and showed off the handsome hairline that bracketed her forehead. It also lifted her eyebrows and blanked out certain subtleties of expression. So who was to know what was in her mind?

Suddenly she said, "I love you, Will."

It struck me dumb. I wanted to tell her I knew that she did. I actually fashioned the words in my heart. But I couldn't make my voice work. I lay on the bed saying nothing.

She said, "Why don't you tell me stories anymore?"

I shook my head.

"I miss them," she said.

None of this was spoken in accusation. Every sentence my sister uttered was the simple statement of a truth.

So this is what I did: I got up and went to the closet and opened the door and picked up the sketchbook and opened it, and showed Debbie the hands and feet and shoulders and wrists on various pages.

"This," I shrugged. "This is what I do now."

"Oh, Willie!" my sister said. She put her hands to her mouth and grinned. "Willie, I never knew you could draw so well."

So it went.

In autumn, Aunt Moravia began to wander the midnight house with her candleflame. She wore nothing but a silken nightgown. She bent low to peer in every dark corner. She wept.

And I wept to hear her.

6.

Once upon a time—just when I started high school and Paul had departed for college—my father told me the story of how his Aunt Moravia came to America by traveling east, not west, from Europe.

He gave his telling the formal sense of a legacy, for he invited me into his private study, he asked me to sit, and he placed between us a heavy, musty album bound in leather.

His Aunt Moravia was a young woman in those days, he told me. She wanted to see Russia. She wanted to see Alaska.

So she made her way ("Sometimes over mud on horse-back," he said, "and often in company of poets.") through Poland to Minsk and Smolensk and finally to Moscow, "Where," Dad said with a restrained delight, "she was the very first woman ever to buy a personal, unchaperoned ticket on the Trans-Siberian Railroad! She took the train from Moscow to Vladivostok. Eight days, and she arrived on the eastern coast of Russia, hardened and unharmed. How bold!" Dad said, gazing off as if he were speaking of his own youth.

That trek was accomplished in the summer of 1907, ten years before my father was born. He knew the story in detail not because anyone in his family had told it to him, but rather because all along the way Aunt Moravia had posted news reports to a newspaper in America. She managed to stir up a little celebrity for herself. It's how she paid for the adventure. And it's how the adventure got preserved.

Dad opened the album and showed me old photos of a woman in voluminous black dresses with football pads for shoulders and buttons up to the throat. Sleeves to the wrist. A hat. Always some huge hat on her head, and slender beauty in her face. Young Moravia had a high, daring set of eyebrows, and Oh!—what a blazing eye! The fire in her eyes destroyed me. They caused a painful contraction in my lower abdomen, which is always the sign of ardor in me.

"I think I know," my father said, "where the writing in you is coming from. You should read your great-aunt's dispatches. The family said she was crazy, a woman too proud and presumptuous, is what they said—but I think she was an artist at heart, an artist born two generations too soon. Your grandfather, my own dad, distanced himself from his sister. So she went to Savannah in Georgia and lived alone until she had to move in with us."

Dad turned the pages of the album slowly.

I saw pictures of Moravia on a wooden packet under wide skies in the Bering Sea. I saw her diminished by mountain slopes behind her. I saw her erect on the docks of Alaska, "Side by side," she reported, "with Wilford B. Hoggatt, appointed last year by President Roosevelt to be governor of the territory. A mining man," she concluded with disdain.

In every picture her posture was unbending, her jaw as firm as bedrock, her person a seeming ice—but her eyes the windows to some interior furnace!

"Why did she go to Savannah, Georgia?"

"The newspaper that printed her travel reports was published there. She planned to keep writing for it."

"Do you have what she wrote then? Can I see it?" Oh, the knowledge kept tugging sweetly in my abdomen: a published writer here, living right here with me!

"No," Dad said.

"Why not? Does someone else have it?"

"No. We have nothing she wrote after coming to America."

"Didn't *she* want to save it? Didn't *she* keep copies?"

"William, there was nothing to save."

"What do you mean?"

"As soon as the editors met your great-aunt Moravia, they realized they had no permanent place for her on the staff. She lacked, they said, the refinement of the women of the South. And she may have written books and books, then, Will. But she never spoke of writing again, and nothing was published."

My father had moved from admiration to wistfulness in the space of twenty minutes.

He said, "I didn't know how poor she was…" He paused. "Or how troubled her mind had become," he said, "until a friend of hers gave me a telephone call. A schoolteacher named Zimmermann. *'Kennen Sie,'* he shouted through the receiver: 'Do you know how highly your aunty speaks of you?'"

7.

By the Thanksgiving of my senior year, I found myself putting the body parts together. Carefully I had begun to draw the entire human, his arms flung up in something like triumph, though the gesture remained ambiguous to me. It could have been fright or shock or simply the act of reaching. I figured I'd find out by the time I fashioned a face and gave it an expression.

On Thanksgiving Day, I watched the football game of

the team which my brother had once enriched with grace and controlled ferocity. I lay on the floor, languid, blank.

Debbie watched the game too. She was in the fifth grade. She kept jumping up to perform cheerleading kicks and to twirl her baton dangerously close to glass and windows and pottery. I didn't say anything. I just let it go.

Two weekends later, on a cold and muffled Saturday morning, Debbie marched into my bedroom and grabbed my hand and pulled me, stumbling, out: out of the room, out of the house, outside.

"Look," she said, white feathery clouds coming from her mouth. "What do you see?"

"That you have no coat on."

"William, *look!*" she said. "It's snowing."

"Yes," I said. "So what?"

She pointed to the white pines that lined our backyard, their arms laden with cold white loads. "It's beautiful, is what," she said.

I looked at the pines. I looked down at Debbie. Her bottom lip was trembling. She was not enjoying the beauty.

She took my hand again and pulled me through the backyard, past the pine-tree border to a woods and a small lake south of us.

"Look and see!" she demanded.

I did. I saw people ice skating in mittens and gloves and flying scarves. I saw a girl dressed in a tight red suit, saw her sailing backward at the speed of fire. Suddenly the skater jammed the teeth of the toe of her blade in the ice, flew upward, and executed an endless spinning in the air before she landed in a grand sweep backward. I tried to memorize her face. I thought of drawing her face at the instant of landing.

But Debbie yanked on my arm with such surprising strength that I lost balance and knelt down in front of her.

No, she was not rejoicing in beauty. She was angry.

"William," she said, "are we going to have a Christmas this year or not? *They* are," she yelled, pointing toward the lake. "*They* are," she yelled again, pointing at the pine trees. "How come we're not?"

"Sure we are," I said.

"Liar," she yelled. "There's no Christmas here. You never talk to me anymore. You're so mad at me," Debbie yelled, the tears beginning to brighten her eyes. "You're so mad at me, and I don't even know why."

"No, I'm not," I said.

"Liar!" she cried.

I said, "You should get a coat on."

"Willie, don't send me away anymore," she shouted, and then the tears came down and her small voice broke. "Please, please, tell me what I did. Why is my brother mad at me?"

"I'll go get us coats," I said.

Debbie grabbed my shirt collars in both her hands. "I don't know what I did," she wept. She was crying very hard. "Willie, what did I do?"

My sister Debbie, my poor little sister, she was lonely. Her dark, narrow face presented such heavy misery that I put my arms around her, and I started to cry too. We both cried.

"I'm not mad at you," I whispered into her ear. I put my cheek against her wet cheek. "If I'm mad," I said, "I think I'm mostly mad at God. Paulie was good, Debbie. He was the best person I have ever known in all my life— and he is the only one I know who has died. Paulie was good. He loved God better than anyone. Why would God let him die? I don't understand."

The snow fell in windless silence.

Debbie was patting my back with one hand.

But we held the embrace and she said, "When we were

in the hospital last year, I prayed for God to let me die instead of Paulie. But God didn't let me die. Paulie died. So Mom and Dad are so sad that they have gone away from us, like they would rather be with him, not us. And you went away, too, and I couldn't stand it, Will. I couldn't stand it without you. But I'm not mad at God. I wish you weren't mad at God too."

I didn't answer.

My sister loved me. This was such heavy, heavy good news that I could not utter a word for a very long time. I just cried, and she kept patting my back.

Soon I felt that she was shivering.

I said, "Let's go in."

She pushed me back in order to look directly into my eyes. Ah, look! There was a Moravian glitter in her eyes and some madness in her glance.

She said, "Will, are we going to have a Christmas?"

I said, "Yes, Deb. Yes, we are. I promise."

So my sister and I formed a small conspiracy.

The closer it got to Christmas, the quieter our parents

became. We were very aware of that. But we took it as a challenge rather than a punishment. We discussed the moods of Mom and Dad, the differences between them, the effect their moods had on us. But we *could* discuss these threatful matters precisely because we were about to break their gloom with gladness. What a surprise our Christmas Eve would be after all!

Well, it didn't occur to Dad to buy a tree that year. So Debbie and I sallied forth on our own, selected a dusty blue spruce, and hid it in the shed behind the garage.

Debbie regularly came to my room now and made ornaments by sticking gluey strips of paper over light bulbs, five thicknesses of strips, and letting them dry. Then she would knock the papier-mâché lightly on my desk, shatter the glass inside, and create rattle-ornaments. I painted them in primary colors.

We bought presents. We made presents. Debbie knitted three separate scarves, for Mom and Dad and Aunt Moravia, while I worked fervently at my drawing.

One evening she stood at my shoulder, watching. I was using pencil on the face, lip corner, lip lines, chin, and the delicate scoop of flesh between.

Suddenly she said, "Oh, I get it. What a good idea, Will. Mom and Dad will love it."

"What?" I said.

"Your picture of Paulie! They'll feel like we're a whole family again. They won't have to go away to find him. Oh, Willie, this will be the very best part of our Christmas."

Paul! I was drawing my brother Paul, and I had not even known it!

For a day or two the knowledge frightened me. What was I doing, really? What did it mean that my mind and my hands and my persistent effort to get things right were *not* mine after all? What was controlling me, and what was me? Debbie was right. The picture was Paul with his arms held high. I felt as if a veil had been snatched away, and there was my brother the instant before he completed a leaping, impossible reception. Ah, that particular moment frightened me, because what was it: triumph or dying?

But then Debbie went through the whole house and gathered up all the pictures of Paul that she could find. She brought them to my closet and arranged them around my little table.

The shock of finding so much Paul in that tiny place accomplished two things. First, by gazing at all his familiar faces I lost my fear of the project. Yes, I could—and yes, I would—make a genuine memorial to my brother, and it would grant me, I believed, a deep and easeful satisfaction.

Second, I made the decision to charm Paul forth from my own heart, from my own love and memory and reverence. In other words, thanks for the pictures, but no thanks, too. I didn't want them near me. I didn't want to see them at all, anywhere. The fixed grins and posed hands must not affect the truer relationship borne forth from my heart and my love. So I stacked all the photos in a cardboard box and tucked them behind old notebooks on a shelf.

Debbie and I planned to adorn the Paul drawing with a subdued wooden frame, and then on Christmas morning to surprise our parents—with gifts, with the blue spruce trimmed, with carols and cookies and prayers and good will, and with love.

It was our dear intent to make of our family a family again.

8.

On the morning of Christmas Eve day, I woke to a nearly animal roaring, hoarse, brutal. Truly, so foreign was the sound that I could not recognize it for half a minute. Then I knew that it was my dad.

He was shouting. I could feel the impact of his heels as he strode back and forth between the living room and the kitchen.

"I swear! I swear," he was bellowing, "I'll break the hand that touched them. I'll break his head for stealing them!"

My stomach went into spasms. I wanted to wretch. I did not know why dad was so enraged. At the same time, I knew. I could figure it out if I really wanted to.

"To hell!" my father thundered. "To HELL with the boy!" So explosive was his passion that I could by the sound alone see it. On *HELL* there was a metallic splat in the kitchen. Dad's keys. He must have had them in his hand. He windmilled his arm and threw them with force to the kitchen floor. "I'm sick and tired of his impertinence, his sanctified attitude, as if he's the only one suffering in this family!"

Me.

He meant me. I'm "the boy."

Suddenly the storm ceased. Debbie's tender voice made murmurs too low for me to interpret. Then Dad shouted, "You tell your thieving brother that they will be back by lunch, or he'll be gone, not Paul. Not the pictures."

The front door slammed so hard I felt it in my bedsprings.

The car engine raced.

The only reason the tires didn't squeal was that Dad was driving on packed snow.

Soon Debbie was rapping on my door. She came in dead white.

"I tried to tell him it was me," she whispered. "Honestly, Willie—but he wouldn't listen. I'm sorry. It's my fault, not yours. It'll be okay. Don't worry, I'll make it okay. Where did you put Paul's pictures, Will? You know, football pictures, graduation pictures? We have to put them back. Why is he so mad? Why is Dad so mad? I've never seen him this mad."

I dressed.

Just as I was hanging the last picture of smiling Paul on the living room wall, I felt ice on the back of my neck. I turned and saw that Mom was staring at me from the kitchen—gaunt, her eyes stricken as if I'd hit her. I began to walk toward her, saying, "We didn't mean any harm—" but she took the hem of her apron and pulled it up to cover her face.

"Mom!" I cried, crushed by her gesture. "Please—"

I would have taken my mother into my arms, but Aunt Moravia appeared between us in the doorframe. Black sockets, marble-white eyeballs, she raised her arm and pointed her forefinger at me. Oh, it was horrible in my heart! It was as if the whole world had passed away, everything except her sepulchral eye and that accusing finger. She did not lower her arm. I backed away. She followed, pointing. I turned and bolted.

Debbie and I spent the morning in the shed outside, trimming the tree. A kerosene heater kept us warm enough. I did not want to go back into the house. Dad came home at noon, spent all of three minutes inside, then left again. There was no joy in me for trimming this tree. But poor Debbie chattered with a hectic need for happiness. She swung in and out of the back door bearing sandwiches and Cokes and cookies. It was for her sake that I spent the day trimming a perfectly shaped, perfectly straight blue spruce Christmas tree.

By six thirty that evening we had all bathed and dressed ourselves in good clothes. Though nothing had actually been said about it on this particular year, it had been our ritual every other year to worship in church on Christmas Eve. Mom had hung a green plastic wreath on the front door of the house. Some customs were still acknowledged in this gloomy household. This one, too. We went to church.

An angel child robed in white declaimed at the top of her lungs: *For unto you. Is born. This day in the city. Of David a Savior which is. Christ the Lord.*

Precious.

Except for my sister Debbie, we were tombstones in the pew. She kept nodding and smiling and patting people's knees—mine, Mother's.

Aunt Moravia had not come with us. During our brief and silent supper she had suddenly arisen, had grabbed herself fore and aft and earnestly supplicated my father, saying, "*Liebling*, can you hear it? Can you hear it?" He did not respond. She asked him twice more whether he could hear the glass piano in her pancreas, her glare growing blacker and more baleful with each appeal. My father remained oblivious. Aunt Moravia picked up her half-eaten hamburger and threw it into his face. Debbie let out a yip. Mom, with no transition, began to weep. Aunt Moravia turned, stalked away, and shut herself in her bedroom. Dad went silently outside to sit in the car until anyone who cared was ready to go to church with him.

And there was! With the angel! A multitude of! The heavenly! Host! Praising…

In my soul a lump has formed, a cancerous mass of resentment. My father swore at me this morning. He cursed me with conviction and no restraint and no apology afterward. He *meant* it! Paul goes to heaven. Me, I'm sent to hell. And here in the pew sits the man who sent me there, his chin raised up, his mouth a sober piety, worshipping God. Yes, I am offended by him. In fact, he has been offending me for an entire year now. I am not responsible for my brother's death. Nor can I *be* my brother. I am William, his second son, somebody who deserves a little time, a little attention, a little recognition, conversation, love, anything, anything. Does he know that I've been accepted at two universities? Does it matter that I'm going to college at all? My whole life has been stunned by the troubles of this year. Me, too! I have died, too! I haven't written a single story in a whole year—

"Will."

—so the truer part of myself has died—

"Willie."

—but no one, absolutely no one—

"William!"

—has noticed.

"What?" I hissed. Debbie was poking me in my side and whispering my name, so that's the reason I said, "What?"

And she said, "Whatever you're doing, stop it. You look like Dad."

Instantly I set my jaw and closed my eyes, furious with my sister.

ANGELS WE HAVE HEARD ON HIGH, SWEETLY SINGING O'ER THE PLAINS, AND THE MOUNTAINS IN REPLY, ECHOING THEIR JOYOUS STRAINS. Glo-ooooo-ooooo-ria IN exCELsis…

After church we drove straight home. We went straight into the house. I watched Mom and Dad. When they had taken their coats off it was pretty clear that they were going straight to bed without a word to us, Dad ascending the stairsteps in grim silence. No cider, no Danish pastries, no talk, no thought for Christmas—not a word at all.

So I said, "If those had been *my* pictures missing, would you have gotten angry then?"

Mom whirled and shot me a frightened glance.

Dad froze mid-step, facing away from me. But by an act of conscious will he took another step, so I shouted: "What's the matter with this house? Do you think we're all dead? Do you think Deb and I are dead, too?"

Mom was panting. "Please, Will, please don't let's talk now. Later, maybe—"

"Oh, Mom!" I yelled. "You know there's never a *later!* Now is now. Now *is* the time to talk. Now is the perfect time—"

My father turned, his eyes enflamed.

He spoke low, with a preternatural calm.

"Paul died," he said. "Not you, William. Paul, my first-born, is dead. This is the day he died. This day, this hour. My dreams, my childhood, my fatherhood, and all my days died with him. It is a father's right to grieve. No one, William—do you hear me?—"

Dad was at the bottom of the stairs. He began to measure slow steps in my direction. I was rooted to the spot.

"No one," he was saying, "knows the pain...of the grief...of a father who has outlived his son—"

I recognized the posture my father's body was taking, balancing on the balls of his feet, the slight crouch in his shoulders, a certain simian crouch that loosened his arms and made them long, bent at the elbow: He was coming to hit me. His muscle and frame were tensing toward the blow, though his mind—exactly like Paul's at the peak of action—had the serenity of a perfect self-assurance. Dad was about to break some bone in my face.

And he was saying softly, "—the grief of a father who has outlived his son. But you! You, so self-absorbed that you refuse to grant me this day, this one day—"

He drew back his right hand.

"—to grieve. Oh, William, who are you to accuse my sorrow?"

Here it came.

But suddenly Aunt Moravia stood between us, facing my father. In a single swift motion she lifted her hand, her hawk's claw, and slapped him. He froze, frowning, still glaring at me. Moravia drew back her hand and slapped him a second time—hard. He turned his glare down to her. He opened his mouth. He retracted his lips and showed his teeth, as if he would spray venom into her eyes.

But she struck him a third time, never altering her death's-head expression: A hanging judge was she.

My father, the left side of his face rose-red, closed his mouth, then turned on his heel and strode to the stairs and ascended them.

Mom, weeping, followed.

Aunt Moravia, changeless, stern, black-eyed, filled with judgment, spun round and raised the accusing finger toward me. "But a prating fool," she said, "shall fall."

That was more than I could take. I rushed away to my own room.

Almost immediately Debbie rapped at my door. "Can I come in?" she called.

I didn't answer.

She came in anyway and had the utter idiocy to say, "Are you ready to bring the tree into the house, Will?"

"Get out," I said. I turned my back on her. "Paul has stolen this Christmas, too," I said. "Get out. Leave me alone."

I threw myself face down on the bed. When I looked again, Debbie was gone.

I stripped to my shorts, switched off the light and crawled under the covers.

Merry Christmas, merry Christmas, merry Christmas. I couldn't sleep. I lay for a very long time, my brains like the dead planets spinning in space, signifying nothing.

Finally I got up and went to my closet and switched on the single bulb above my table. I sat down and began again to draw.

The eyes: like my mother's when yet she was glad, so long, so long ago. Sunlight on the triangle of the left cheekbone, head raised high, eyes already catching the pass the hands must wait for. Much of this—the cheek structure, the bridge of the nose—like my father's, though I had not known *how* much until this very evening's encounter. I was doing the final shading with the edge of my pencil. I was discovering what my hand knew and my head had not. I was watching my brother appear before me. And I was crying because it was him and he was coming to be with me. It was Paul. Here was Paul, in the joining of the skills of our two hands, alive.

Suddenly the light flickered. Yellow shadows jumped

around me. I smelled candleflame, and in the same instant felt drops of hot wax on the back of my neck. I nearly cried out in pain, but the drops were not hot, after all. They were warm. They were tears.

I turned and saw Aunt Moravia in her silken night-gown, her lashless, undefended eyes, weeping, weeping tears all down her wrinkled cheeks.

She was looking at the portrait of my brother Paul.

"Wilhelmus," she whispered in a trembling awe, "Wilhelmus, you have found him! *Lobe den Herren,* and I never need seek him again. He is right here."

Never before had my great-aunt initiated our embraces. But on this night she knelt down beside my chair and set her candlestick on the floor. She put her right arm around the small of my back, her left arm around my knees, and she laid her head upon my lap.

"Wilhelmus, you have found him and taken my loneliness away. I love you, *Enkel.* There is not a better gift to be given to an old woman before she dies."

I began to stroke her thin hair. "I love you, too, Aunty," I said. I meant it. Oh, what this old woman had bequeathed me! Such praise, such sudden kinship. All the walls were down, and she was tender in my lap, as light as a child.

"Maybe my father will be as glad as you. What do you think? Because I brought Paulie home again."

Moravia raised her head and gazed into my eyes.

"Oh, *Liebling,* it isn't Paul can heal my dreariness," she whispered.

Not Paul?

"This is him whom I was seeking," she whispered, her black eyes flashing. "Wilhelmus, this is the Son of God."

9.

I found Debbie asleep in the shed by the Christmas tree. Ah, my darling, so sad, so cold! How sorry I am for wounding you.

I returned to the house and brought out sleeping bags, flashlights, a Coleman stove, fry pan, utensils, bacon, eggs, tangerines, cookies. As quietly as I could, I opened one of the sleeping bags and slipped it under my sister, then zipped it to the second bag and crawled in beside her in order to warm her up.

Just before I fell asleep, I felt her small hand patting my back.

"What are we doing?" she murmured.

"Camping," I said. "We're camping together."

10.

On Christmas morning this is what woke us: Aunt Moravia, shrieking a mighty shriek, screaming the *Laudamus* from the Mass in B Minor by Johann Sebastian Bach. The woman had thrown a window open to the world!

Right away I lit the stove and heated the pan and began to strip the bacon for frying. Debbie gazed up at me from the folds of her sleeping bag, hazy with slumber, grinning at me precisely like a toothless infant.

"Merry Christmas, partner," I whispered. "Watch."

I knelt. I found the end of a long electric cord that I had trailed from the house last night, and I connected it to a small green plug. The Christmas tree burst into light.

"Oh, Will," Debbie cried, dazzled. "Oh, Willie!"

Abruptly, in the middle of a high note, Moravia stopped singing.

Another voice was rumbling in the house. Dad's. I lost

my smile and leaped to protect my sister's peace. Silly fool: I threw the bacon into the pan to cause a spitting hiss. I wanted a sound to drown our father's voice. I wanted to raise a breakfast aroma, the scent that wakes us to goodness and banishes nightmares.

But Dad was saying, "—not in their rooms! Neither one! Both of them gone!" Emotion increased his volume. He was slurring toward some kind of panic. "Moravia! My children are *gone!*"

Debbie and I looked at each other, holding still, scarcely breathing—as if we were suddenly guilty and hiding.

In sharp command, Aunt Moravia uttered the words, *"Komme, Neffe!"*

Come, nephew.

Then a window bumped shut, and silence filled the morning.

The bacon was gurgling, shrinking, crinkling. I plucked it out with a fork. I cracked eggs one after the other and slipped them, yolk and liquid, into the grease.

At the same time a new song arose in the morning, soft and sweet and close, in perfect pitch: Debbie! My sister, glancing from me to the Christmas tree with a dogged purpose, had begun to sing, "Silent night, holy night, all is calm, all is bright—"

Ah, child of the dark and glittering eye, I hear you. I understand: Yes! We will make a Christmas together.

She sang through all three verses.

I filled two metal plates with the food of good camping and two tangerines to signify the holiday.

As I set one between the humps of her legs in the sleeping bag, Debbie touched the back of my hand and concluded the carol expressly for me: "Jesus, Lord, at your birth; Jesus, Lord, at your—"

All at once the same carol exploded right outside the door of our fortress. But in German. And in a shattering contralto: *"Stille Nacht, heilige Nacht! Alles schlaft, einsam wacht—nur das heilige Elternpaar…"*

There came a knocking hard enough to shake the shed.

Aunt Moravia cried at the top of her lungs (in rage? in haste? Or what?—in joy?), *"Ein Elternpaar!"*—which means something like, "A pair of parents!"

Debbie whispered, "It's okay, Willie."

So I opened the door. Moravia, lifting her thin lip over those long yellow incisors, jumped to the side, and there was my father, pale, pained, searching my face with a fierce intensity. "William?" Flat on his outstretched hands, as if it were a silver platter, he was carrying the pencil-sketch of my brother. My mother stood beside him, weeping—but weeping with a helpless smile and nodding at us, nodding at Debbie and me.

"Hinein!" Moravia snapped: "Get in there!"

They crowded into the shed, all three.

I retreated, feeling awkward: like a host caught empty-handed. "Want some"—I shrugged—"eggs?"

"William," Dad murmured, gazing at me so intently that my face grew warm. "Did you make this…drawing?"

Cautiously: "Yes."

"Really?" he said. He cocked his head; he narrowed his eyelids for a new perspective. "*You* did this? You brought Paul to paper?"

I didn't answer. I had already answered. I shrugged.

Dad lowered his gaze to the portrait between us. He took two trembling breaths. "Paul," he said, "Paul…had his mother's eyes."

Mom, smiling a moist, glittering smile, repeated: "My

eyes. My eyes. And you're the one, Sweet William, who saw it."

"And these...hands...reaching for the football—" Dad said slowly: "They're my hands, aren't they?"

Debbie had risen from the sleeping bag. She moved past me to Dad's side. "And Paulie had your cheek," she said, touching his face with the tips of her fingers. "Your nose. Your jaw. Your chin."

Dad inclined his head toward Debbie's hand and brushed the knuckles with his lips. Suddenly his face went slack, and he heaved a noisy sob.

Moravia interrupted. *"Liebling,"* she whispered, "can you hear it?"

In tight quarters, Dad glanced at her, then bent his forehead and laid it on his old aunt's shoulder. "I hear it," he murmured. "Ah, *Tante,* I have always heard it."

I said nothing, but I swear I heard it too, issuing from Moravia's mouth: a tiny tinkling, like the kiss of ice crystals or the cries of Alaskan damselflies or the touch of glassy piano keys producing trills for songs to come.

Songs to come:

Moravia raised her hawk's-claw hand, cradled her nephew's head, and pressed his cheek against her own. She closed her eyes and, in a voice as soft as my sister's, sang to the sounds of the glass piano: *"Der heilge Christ ist kommen—In tiefer Winternacht—"*

Which means something like: "The Son of God has come among us."

To my amazement my father murmured the second verse of that hymn in Moravia's ear and in her mother tongue: *"Zu Bethlehem im Stalle, Ein Kindlein zart und klein, Nicht in der Konigshalle—"*

Which means something like: "Not in the big house, but here in the shed."

"Will?" Deb whispered, tugging my elbow.

"What?"

"You see?"

Ah, my sister, this is what I see: that you are a fresh Moravia, flashing glee and packing your bags for a very long journey.

"You see?" she whispered close beside me. "We did it. We made a Christmas after all."

THE CAROL OF THE SEVEN SIGNS

Marye, maide milde and fre,
Chambre of the trinite,
Icrouned and ilore…

i

The brier in a dry land grows;
Mary shall wear the bloodred rose,
Her son shall wear the thorn.

ii

Saint Joseph cut the cherry tree
Whose fruit he gave to his lady.
Then what was left? The stone.

Saint Joseph cut mahogany
To make the babe a crib—but he
    Was to the manger born,
    To wood already worn.

One father split the cedar tree
And made two beams: "A house!" cried he;
    "A cross," the other mourned.

iii

Shepherds brought wool to the royal stall,
For the mother a robe, for her darling a pall,
    For their sleeping, both cold and warm.

Three gentlemen offered three measures of myrrh,
A drop to perfume, a sponge to blur,
    A tun to embalm the Lord.

And gold is lovely to the eye
But cold as stone to him who lies
    Behind the golden door.

iv

Now these—the brier and the cherry,
Wood and wool and gold—did Mary
 Ponder when Christ was born.

Within her heart she kept it all,
A thorn, a cross, a stone, a pall,
 And they herself adorned—

For the pain was his, but he was hers,
Her child, the treasure in her purse,
 By whom her womb was torn,
 Et eius Salvator.

A Quiet Chamber
Kept for Thee

This is the way it was in the old days:

The milkman still delivered milk to our back door, summer and winter. The milk came in bottles, and the bottles were shaped with a bulge at the top for the cream, you see, which separated after the fluid had been bottled. Cream was common in those days. So was butter. Margarine was less appealing because, according to Canadian law, it had to be sold in its original color, which was white like lard, and could be colored yellow only by the customer after she had bought it. Or so my mother told me. She mixed an orange powder into the margarine to make it butter-yellow.

But this is the way it was in the old days:

The milkman still carried his wares in a horse-drawn

wagon, arriving at our house in the middle of the morning. And especially in the winter we would, as my mother said, "tune our ears to hear his coming." That is, we listened for the kindly, congregational clinking of the glass as his wagon toiled down our particular street, and then we rushed to an upstairs window and watched. In the cold Canadian air, you could hear his coming from far away. We were breathing on the window long before the milkman came bustling up our walk with bottles in a wire basket. And that, of course, was the point: My mother wanted us to bring the milk in right away or else it would freeze, and the cream would lift its hat on an ice-cream column:

"How-do-you-do?"

"Fine, thank you, Mr. Cream, and how are you?"

But this is the way it was, especially on Christmas Eve day:

We spent the major portion of the morning at the upstairs window, giggling, whispering, and waiting for the milkman to come. Tradition. My mother was glad to be shed of us on the day she "ran crazy" with preparations. I think we knew that then. But for our own part, we did truly want to see some evidence of how cold it was outside. It was important that Christmas Eve be cold. And it was the milkman's mare, you see, who presented us with evidence.

So here came the mare in a slow walk, nodding, drawing the wagon behind her even when her master was rushing up sidewalks, making deliveries. She never stopped. And the mare was blowing plumes of steam from her nostrils. Her chin had grown a beard of hoarfrost. Her back was blanketed. The blanket smoked. The air was cold. The air was very cold, and our stomachs contracted with joy within us, and some of us laughed at the rightness of the weather. So here came the mare, treading a hardened snow. The snow banked six feet high on either side of the street, except at sidewalks and driveways. The snow was castles we would be kings of tomorrow. The snow collected on the mare, whose forelock and eyelashes were white. She shivered the flesh on her flanks, sending off small showers of snow. And so did we—shiver. Ah, cold! The air was a crystal bowl of cold! The day was perfectly right.

And we could scarcely stand our excitement.

Downstairs, directly below us in the house, was a room that had been locked two days ago against our entering in. This was my father's tradition, which he never varied year to year. Always, he locked the door by removing its knob, transfiguring thereby the very spirit of the room; all we could do was spy at the knob-hole and wonder at the mysteries concealed inside. My brothers and sisters pestered that hole continually, chirping among themselves, puffing their imaginations like feathers all around themselves.

Tonight, on Christmas Eve itself, we would all line up, and my father would slip the knob back into the door, and one by one we would enter the wondrous room. This much we knew: The Christmas tree was in there.

Therefore, even in the morning at the upstairs window, we could scarcely stand the excitement.

Tonight! And lo: It was very, very cold.

Let me be more specific.

We were living in Edmonton, Alberta, then. The year was 1954, and I was ten, the oldest of seven children. I've implied that we were all excited on that particular Christmas Eve morning, and so we were; but though my brothers and sisters could manifest their excitement with unbridled delight, I could not mine. I absolutely refused to acknowledge or signal excitement. They loved the sweet contractions in their stomachs. I was afraid of them. For I had that very year become an adult: silent, solemn, watchful, and infinitely cautious.

So my brothers and sisters laughed and clapped the day away. They spilled colored sugar on cookie dough and covered the kitchen table with a sweet mess, all unworried, unafraid. They claimed, by faster stabs of the finger, their individual treasures from Sears catalogs, and so they allowed their dreams to soar, and so they passed the day. I didn't blame them. They were innocent; they could dare the dangers they didn't see. These children could rush headlong toward the evening, recklessly. But I could not.

I held myself in a severe restraint. Because—what if you hope, and it doesn't happen? It's treacherous to hope. The harder you hope, the more vulnerable you become. And what if you believe a thing, but it isn't true? Well, the instant you see the deception, you die a little. And it hurts in your soul exactly where once you had believed. I knew all this. I had learned that excitement is composed of hope and faith together—but of a faith and a hope in promises yet unkept—and I was not about to let excitement run away with me, or else I would certainly crash as I had crashed last year.

Last Christmas Eve in the midst of opening his presents, my brother Paul had burst into tears. I didn't know—and I don't know—why. But I was shocked to discover that the Christmas time is not inviolate. I was horrified that pain could invade the holy ceremony. And I was angry that my father had not protected my brother from tears. There was a fraud here. The traditions of merry gentlemen and gladness and joy were as thin as a crystal globe and empty. I could do nothing about that, of course, when I was nine years old, nothing but sob in an ignorant sympathy with my brother, nothing but grieve to the same degree as I had believed.

But by ten I was an adult. And if Christmas gave me nothing really, and if the traditions could not protect me from assault, then I would protect myself.

No: The more excited I was, the more I was determined not to be, and the more I molded my face into a frown.

I'm speaking with precision now. None of us could stand the season's excitement. But I was frightened by mine and chose to show it to no one, not to my father, not to my mother, and not to myself.

Adult.

By supper the world was black outside, so the noise inside seemed louder than it had been, and we the closer together. In bathrobes we ate soup. We had bathed: bright faces, soft faces, sparkling eyes in faces glowing with their soulful goodness. My brothers and sisters ran to their bedrooms, bubbling, and began to dress themselves.

I stood before the bathroom mirror and combed my hair with water, unsmiling.

Always we went to church on Christmas Eve to participate in the children's service. Nothing happened at home till after that. This was the tradition; and tradition itself began when we would venture into the cold, cold night, on our way to perform the parts we had been practicing for endless Saturdays. And if we were nervous about the lines we had to say, well, that only intensified excitement for the time thereafter: the room, the mystery, and the tree.

My hair froze as soon as I walked outside. It crackled when I touched it. It felt like a cap. Cold.

My face tightened in the night wind, and I blew ghosts of steam that the wind took from my lips. They were leaving me and wouldn't come back again.

The family sat three, three, and three in the three seats of a Volkswagen van, I in the farthest corner of the back, slouched, my hands stuffed in my pockets. I forced myself to repeat my lines for the pageant. I was to be Isaiah.

So then it was a blazing church we crowded into, a small church filled with yellow light and stifling excitement. People were laughing simply at the sights of one another, as though familiar faces were a fine hilarity: "You, Harold, ha-ha-ha! *You!*"

In the narthex the press of people squashed us because we wore thick coats; and the children were shooed downstairs to giddy into costumes, and the adults clumped upstairs to wait in pews, and holly greens were knocked from the windowsills, and the windows were black with night. Who is so foolish as to laugh in such an atmosphere and not to fear that he's losing control?

Not me.

Class by class the children tromped into the chancel. As the pageant proceeded, they sang with wide-open mouths all full of faith, eyes unafraid. The little ones waved to their parents by the crooking of four fingers, like scratching the air. They positively shined for happiness. No one thought to be fearful.

I, in my turn, stared solemnly at the massed congregation and intoned: "For unto us a child is born, unto us a son."

I saw the adults jammed shoulder to shoulder in ranks before me, nodding and craning, encouraging me by grins, not a whit afraid.

"Wonderful, Counselor—"

No one was ready to sob in the midst of so much cheer and danger. Naive people—or else they were cunning. Well, neither would I.

"Mighty God!" I roared.

I would not cry. Neither would I succumb to the grins of these parents, no.

"Everlasting Father!"

Oh, no, I would not risk disappointment again this year.

"The Prince of Peace!" I thundered, and I quit.

No emotion whatsoever. I did not laugh. I did not smile. Both of these are treacherous lapses. I made a glowering prophet altogether. My father and my mother sat nearly hidden ten rows back. I noticed them just before descending from the chancel.

Walnuts, tangerines, a curled rock candy all in a small brown bag—and every kid got a bag at the end of the service. A bag was thrust toward me too, and I took it, but I didn't giggle and I didn't open it. *No sir! You won't entice me to gladness or gratitude.*

And the people, humping into coats again, called, "Merry Christmas! Merry Christmas!"—the pleasant tumult of departure. They were flowing outward into the black night, tossing goodwill over their shoulders like peanuts: "Merry Christmas!" *No ma'am! You won't disarm me again this year.*

Even now my father delayed our going home. Tradition. As long as I can remember, my father found ways to while the time, increasing excitement until his children fairly panted piety and almost swooned in their protracted goodness.

"Don't breathe through your noses," my father sang out, hunched at the wheel of the van. This was his traditional joke. "You'll steam the windows," he called. "Breathe through your ears."

Silliness.

We breathed through our noses anyway, frosting the windows a quarter-inch thick, enclosing our family in a cave of space in the night. With mittened knuckles and elbows we rubbed peepholes through the muzzy ice. We were driving through the city to view its Christmas decorations, lights and trees and stables and beasts and effigies of the Holy Family. This, too, was tradition.

I peered out my little hole and regarded the scenes with sadness.

There was a tremendous tableau of Dickensian carolers in someone's yard, some dozen singers in tall hats and scarves and muffs, their mouths wide open, their eyes screwed up to heaven in a transport of song—their bodies a wooden fiction. Two-dimensioned plywood. They didn't move. They didn't produce a note of music. So nobody heard them. But nobody minded. Because no one was singing. And not a living soul was anywhere near them anyway. Except us, passing at the behest of my humorous father.

This was worse than silliness. This was dangerous. I found myself suddenly full of pity for the wooden figures and their plaintive gladness—as though they could be lonely in the deserted snow. Any feeling at all, you see, made me vulnerable. I stopped looking.

My boots crunched dry snow when we walked to the door of our house. A wind with crystals caused my eyes to tear. But resolutely, I was not crying.

And still my father delayed our going into the room.

Oh, who could control the spasms of his excitement? Dad! Dad, let's *do* it and be done!

But it was tradition, upon returning home, that we change from our church clothes into pajamas and then gather in the kitchen.

Across the hall the door was still closed—but its knob had been replaced. I saw that knob, and my heart kicked inside of me. So I chewed my bottom lip and frowned like thunder. *No! It won't be what it ought to be. It never is.*

Adult.

And always, always the hoops of my father's tradition: We line up in the kitchen from the youngest to the oldest. I stood last in a line of seven. My little sister Dena was clasping her hands and raising her shining, saintly face to my father, who stood in front of her, facing us all. Her hair hung down her back to the waist. Blithe child! Her blue eyes burst with trust. I pitied her.

My father prayed a prayer, tormenting me. For the prayer evoked the very images I was refusing: infant Jesus, gift of God, love come down from heaven—all the things that conspired to make me glad at Christmas. My poor heart bucked and disputed that prayer. No! I would not hope. No! I would not permit excitement. No! No! I would not be set up for another disappointment!

We were a single minute from entering the room.

And I might have succeeded at severity—

—except that then we sang a song, the same song we had always sung, and the singing undid me altogether. Music destroys me. A hymn can reduce me to infancy.

Nine bare voices, unaccompanied in the kitchen,

we sang: *Ah, dearest Jesus, holy child*—and I began to tremble. *Make thee a bed, soft, undefiled*— The very sweetness of the melody caused my defenses to fall: I began to hope, and I began to fear, both at once. I began to wish, and wishing made me terrified. I began all over again to believe, but I had never ceased my unbelief. I began to panic.

—*Within my heart; that it may be*—

Dreadfully, now, I yearned for some good thing to be found in that room, but "dreadfully" because I was an adult; I had put away childish things; I had been disillusioned and knew no good to be in there at all. This was a pitiless sham!

—*A quiet chamber kept for thee.*

My father whispered, "Now."

He turned to the door.

Little squeals escaped my sister.

He grasped the knob and opened the door upon a muted, colored light; and one by one his children crept through the doorway, looking, not breathing.

There, shedding a dim and varied light, was the Christmas tree my father had decorated alone, every single strand of tinsel hanging straight down of its own slim weight since he draped them individually, patiently, never hastening the duty by tossing tinsel in fistfuls (tradition!)—the tree that he had hidden three days ago behind a knobless door.

There, in various places around the room, were seven piles of presents, a pile for each of us.

There, in the midst of them, my mother sat smiling on the floor, her skirts encircling her, her radiance smiting my eyes, for she verged on laughter. My mother always laughed when she gave gifts, however long the day had been, however crazy she had almost gone.

I began to blink rapidly.

But there, unaccountably, was my father, standing center in the room and gazing straight at me. At me. And this is the wonder fixed in my memory forever: that the man himself was filled with a yearning, painful expectation; but that he, like me, was withholding still his own excitement—on account of *me.*

Everything else in this room was just as it had been the year before, and the year before that. But this was new. This thing I had never seen before: that my father, too, had passed his day in the hope that risks a violent hurt. My father, too, had had to trust the promises against their disappointments. So said his eyes still steadfast on me. But among the promises to which my father had committed his soul, his hope, and his faith, the most important one was this: that his eldest son should soften and be glad.

If I had grown adult in 1954, then lo how like a child my father had become!

The colored lights painted the side of his face. He gazed at me, waiting, waiting for me, waiting for his Christmas to be received by his son and returned to him again.

And I began to cry.

O my father!

Silently, merely spilling the tears and staring straight back at him, defenseless because there was no need for defenses, I cried—glad and unashamed. Because, what *was* this room, for so long locked, which I was entering now? Why, it was my own heart. And why had I been afraid? Because I thought I'd find it empty, a hard, unfeeling thing.

But there, in the room, was my father.

And there, in my father, was the love that had furnished this room, preparing it for us no differently than he had last year, yet trusting and yearning, desiring our joy.

And what else could such a love be but my Jesus drawing near to me?

Look, then, what I have found in my father's room, in my heart after all: the dearest Lord Jesus, holy child—

The nativity of our Lord.

I leaned my cheek against the doorjamb and grinned like a grownup ten years old, and sobbed as if I were two. And my father moved from the middle of the room and walked toward me, still empty-handed; but he spread his arms and gathered me to himself. And I put my arms around his harder body. And so we, both of us, were full.

This is the way that it was in the olden days.

THE CAROL
OF ALL THE
INSTRUMENTS

i

Whistle on wooden pipes:
    Wake the children!
    Wake the children!
Plead on a wailing reed
That the children arise and come.

ii

Organ, send forth a chord
    Through the morning
    And their sleeping;
Pour in their souls the gold
Of the light of the rising sun.

iii

Bugle! Oh, bugle the news
   Last night, midnight
   Stall and stable…
Bells-bells, declaim the news:
Lo, a baby was born! A Son!

iv

Bass drum and snare drum, march
   Straight to the stable
   Leading children,
Sounding their footfalls, march,
That the baby can hear them come.

v

Gabriel, greet them now,
   Whisper *Welcome,*
   All ye children;
Angels, ignite the sky
With the fires of a midnight crown.

vi

Orchestras! Angels! Choirs!
    Raise a roaring:
    Glory! Glory!
Children, now round your mouths
To give praise in ten thousand tongues!

vii

King and his crown are here,
    Born in glory,
    Cradled poorly,
Baby shall grow to bear
On his forehead the thorns of wrong.

viii

Jesus! One flute alone,
    Silver singing
    Sings to children,
Flute of five stops, his song:
I will love you till day is done—

ix

Love you until that night,
*   Night of dying,*
*   Dies in rising!*
Then in the holy dawn
I will bear you, my children, home,
In my bosom, the whole way home.

THE EVENING
FOR GIVING

Three times in the middle of a single night, Gertrude
Weiss heard someone crying. Three times the sound
of it woke her from sleeping. And every time, the crying
was so much sadder than the time before that each time
seemed the *only* time Gertrude heard it.

A high and lonesome wailing came into Gertrude's ears, a
cry as thin as a string, and she woke. It must have been a
baby—so sad, so sad that Gertrude felt as if she were the
one that had been crying in her sleep. But when she sat up,
she could tell that the sound was coming from outside the
house.

Gertrude stood on her feather tick, breathing ghosts in the cold, and climbed the loft-ladder down. It was no warmer below than above. Had her father forgotten to bank the woodstove fire? But she couldn't wait.

Ooooo, oooo! The pitiful little wailing was ceaseless.

She ran out on the back stoop, and turned her head left and right in the night, and learned that the crying came from the barn. The baby must be in the barn.

Gertrude knew better than to think it was a cat making that sound, for though a cat can yowl and complain like a baby, a cat is never sad.

Ooooo, oooo! Oh, listen to the misery in that thin little voice! Hurry, Gertrude! Hurry!

This was the eleventh winter of her life, the coldest Gertrude had ever known; yet she did not stop for a coat or shoes. She went down the back steps barefoot, wearing nothing but a woolen gown and her long, long hair. She ran the beaten snow between the house and the barn, never feeling the sting of the ice on her feet, for this was a night of purest mystery.

Her father had built their little house six years ago.

But first he had built the barn, so the family had to live in a house whose walls were sod and whose roof was thatch. Her father said that the sheep were their future, and the horses his strength—and there weren't big trees on the prairie. Lumber came, as did all exotic things, by wagons from the east. Very expensive. So the first boards built a barn to protect their little flock from bitterest weather.

And this was weather more bitter than devil spit!

Yes, of course: Gertrude could surely understand why someone would try to find shelter for a baby tonight. Her only surprise was, *Why didn't they come to the house?*

The girl ran on bare feet over the snow, her long hair streaming black behind her. She lifted the bar that bolted the big doors from its brackets and dropped it and with her whole body-strength pulled one of the doors open.

"Hello?" she called, creeping in. It was darker here than outside over snow. "Can I help you with your baby?"

Nobody answered.

But the baby wailed with earnest sadness, *Ooooo, oooo!* Tiny weeping, tiny troubles!—the sound of it came from the haymow overhead.

Gertrude heard one of the horses nicker a greeting and stamp his heavy hoof.

"Not you, Balthazar," she said. "Not you either," she

said to the ewes now rustling in straw. "It's the baby I've come to help."

She raised her face and her voice, and sang out as confidently as she could: "Hello? Hello? Who's there, please?"

Well, it could have been a Dakota family, or maybe the Gypsies her grandmother talked about.

Ooooo, oooo! the baby cried, but no one else answered.

So Gertrude took a very big breath and began to climb the wooden rungs her father had built against the wall.

Not that the haymow made her afraid. She played there often with dolls and Caspar's kittens and the balls a tinker once brought by. But company was unusual, and most people knocked at the house first.

The animals kept the stalls warm below; but the air in the mow was cold, cold.

Gertrude climbed up through a framed hole and peeped over the great sheaves of hay her father had bound together and piled up here.

It seemed she could see a vague reflection of light against the ceiling beams.

"Hello?"

And then there was the slightest ghostly glow in a higher pocket of hay.

Gertrude crawled on her hands and knees up to the top of a hay hill and looked down—

Yes! There was indeed a tiny baby there, but all alone! It was lying on a linen blanket so bright it seemed to shed a shadowy sort of light. *Oh, baby! Oh, poor baby! It breaks my heart to see how sorrowful your little face is, your chin trembling, your eyebrows lifted in bewildered disappointment.*

"Who would leave you here?" Gertrude whispered. *Whoever could abandon a baby anywhere, anytime—but especially on this night?*

She crawled closer to the baby on its blanket. Its weeping suddenly stopped. The infant stared at big Gertrude, descending.

"No, no, don't be scared of me," she sang softly. By chance, her hand bumped one of her wooden balls in the hay.

"Here," she said, smiling, trying to make herself look like a very pleasant and trustworthy person. "See? A little ball to play with. Do you want it?"

As she spoke, Gertrude shook back her hair, brought her legs around, and sat facing the baby, who stared at her with its lips parted as if to smile. She put her hand up. In her hand was the wooden ball.

The tiny baby saw the ball and, yes: smiled. A toothless, dimpled, wide-eyed smile.

Gertrude was delighted

"Really?" she said. "Do you like my ball?"

The baby raised its little right hand. Gertrude leaned and reached the ball forward. The baby opened all five fingers very wide and, with a swift skill, took the ball.

Gertrude gasped.

As soon as the infant took the ball, as soon as Gertrude released it, it changed. The ball was transfigured. The wooden ball turned into gold, a polished gold, a gold so glorious that in the baby's hand it shined with its own light, brighter and brighter.

The face of the baby grew very grave—not sad anymore, but knowing and full of knowledge. It shined, now, as golden and as bright as the ball. Rays of sunlight shot forth from the baby's head, causing Gertrude to think that he was wearing a golden crown.

From the midst of an impossible light, the infant gazed straight at Gertrude. Then he nodded, as if to say, *All is well now. All the world is very well.*

And so it was that she must have fallen back to sleep, so swiftly that she could not recall the falling.

In the middle of a bitter winter's night, Gertrude Weiss—no more than eleven years old, yet burdened already by the remembrance of some great sorrow—woke up to the sound of a grievous weeping.

She touched her throat, because it ached as if she had been crying. She touched her eyes, because they seemed swollen with tears.

No, but the *real* weeping, the sound that had awoken her, was outside the house and very clear. It was a child's voice, and every time the child drew breath to cry again, the breath itself was shivering.

Oh-hhhh! the child wept. The sound could have been the wind on that fearfully freezing night: *Oh-hhhh!* But Gertrude knew better, for shivering means coldness and crying means pain, and though the wind grows very cold, it never suffers from it.

Gertrude arose on her feather tick and hurried down the loft-ladder. Down she went on lightsome feet, quickly to the woodstove, where the fire was glowing, rosy and well banked.

Next to it was a lamp with a good glass chimney, very precious, for it had come from east of the east, from the old country with her grandmother when *she* was a girl; and the oil in this lamp had not been rendered from anyone's hog; it was bought!

Gertrude made a great knot of her long hair in order to keep it from singeing, then took a wand of woven straw and opened the woodstove and touched the straw to coals until it flamed. She lifted the glass of the precious lamp and caught its wick on fire.

Holding it high over her head, Gertrude ran outside on bare feet and stood very, very still. *Oh, bitter wind, stop blowing! Be still, as still as Gertrude, that she might hear whence this freezing weeping comes.*

The lamp she carried made but a little light in the blizzard night, its flame the glimmer of a single star. The wind strove to put it out, but Gertrude turned her back to the wind and protected the fire with her own body.

Oh-hhhh! Cold! There it was: The shivering cries were coming from the barn.

Gertrude traveled the snow-path to the big doors of the barn. She raised the bar that shut them tight, suffering the chill in the child's crying, longing to give comfort, to console the cold with a little heat.

She pulled one door wide open. There came upon her

the dear rush of animal heat and animal odor, rich and beloving. A cat crept toward her ankle.

"No, no, Caspar," she said, walking into the darkness, causing great shadows to flee before her. "It's the child! It's the child that needs me now!"

The crying was in the haymow.

Gertrude climbed the mow-ladder with one hand, carefully holding the precious lamp above her.

So the flame arose in the cavernous mow before the girl did, and the child's crying seemed to soften. But the girl soon followed. She was a nimble child, was Gertrude. Lightly she ascended the mountains of hay, and swiftly down toward a hidden valley. She could see, for wasn't she carrying her own light with her? Yes, she could see in that valley a boy about her age, skinny, bony, crouched in rags, his fingers blue and his lips pale blue with the cold.

She didn't recognize him. He must have traveled very far, then, since the farms on the prairie were spaced great distances apart—and those were neighbors Gertrude knew.

The boy, shivering, lifted his eyes and looked at Gertrude. *Oh, lad, thine eyes are huge with affliction! Ghostly, they are, with the cold!* The girl's hand flew to her throat, for the boy's eyes were the dark roads of the spirit's journeys.

"I'm sorry," she whispered. "I'm sorry you're so cold."

She knelt down in the hay before him so that their faces came to the same level, the flaming wick held up between. "Do you want to go into the house?" she said.

He didn't answer. *Oh, why, lad? Why must thou by thy seeing search me to the soul?* Instead, he pointed at the lamp.

"It's warm," said Gertrude, smiling. "It's very warm."

Slowly, the boy rose up on his own knees and extended his right hand toward the lamp. Noble was his motion, straight his spine, elevated his jaw and all his aspect. There appeared a regality in his posture. Therefore, when he reached toward the lamp, Gertrude held it out for him, and he took it.

When he took it, the fire flared so bright that the lamp became a shadow, a darkness, a nothing.

But the flame remained, burning, sparking, smoking in the palm of the lad's right hand! What a thick smoke it poured forth!—smoke as white as a veil between the boy and the girl.

Gertrude cried out, "What are you doing?"

The boy said right clearly, "Can't you smell it, my darling?"

Yes! Oh, yes: The smoke was scented! So sweetly pungent was the taste of it, that it caused her mouth to water.

Aromatic smoke, it smelled scarlet, like her mother's breath when she returned from receiving holy communion. It smelled like the wild onions of springtime, crushed under children's feet when they came running. It smelled like Dakota sage, sparkling on rocks so hot they glowed. It smelled like wood from the East, the farthest of all the farther easts, where trees grow gnarled and weep tears of a bitter beauty. It smelled like the prayers of her parents.

White and thick and warm was the billowing smoke. It surrounded Gertrude and entered her lungs, and her limbs grew heavy, and the deep parts of her mind relaxed into a perfect serenity, and she fell asleep.

When Gertrude Weiss—the only child on this particular farm on the flat and everlasting prairie—was awoken in the middle of a winter's night by a terrible groaning, she almost believed that she had heard nothing at all.

Gertrude lay on her feather tick and listened with all her might.

There! Yes, there it was—but only barely there. Oh, how piteously low was that groaning! Weak. There was no strength in it. And it sounded so injured, that Gertrude Weiss herself was crying.

Tears ran from her eyes and down her temples and into the little cups of her ears. She could not stop them, for she felt as helpless as the poor soul groaning outside. What could she do?

Gertrude crept on her hands and knees to the loft-ladder and turned and descended.

What could an eleven-year-old girl do? The groaning outside was so faint and failing, that it seemed the sound of someone dying!

She crept to her parents' room.

She rapped lightly on the rough wooden door. No one answered. So she pushed the door inward and tiptoed to the side of their bed.

"Papa," she whispered. "Papa, wake up."

But he was sleeping the sleep of Adam. He didn't stir. He couldn't hear her.

She went to the other side of the bed and put her hand on her mother's shoulder. "Mama? Mama?" Gertrude shook the woman, sobbing convulsively. *Mama, please! These groanings are tearing my heart in two, but what can I do for the dying? Mama, Mama, help me, please!*

But her mother was sleeping as deeply as the soil beneath the snow. Neither did she awaken.

Yet outside their little house, the groanings had dwindled down to sighs, a mere and hollow gasping.

So Gertrude went out alone.

Nothing in her hands.

Nothing on her feet.

Just herself, a child in a white woolen nightgown whose tears were freezing to her lashes.

Where was the gasping coming from?

By the barn. In a drift of snow blown up by the big doors of the barn.

As the wind tugged her nightgown and made a great black sail of her long hair, Gertrude walked slowly toward that drift. She saw a hole in it the length of a human body.

And then she saw the body.

Here lay a man on his side in the snow. It seemed that he had tried to make it into the barn, for the beam that kept the barn doors shut had fallen across his skull. He must have lifted it, then collapsed beneath its weight.

He was wounded. The flesh of his forehead had been laid open by the edge of the beam, and he had already bled such a wide patch of blood into the snow, that

Gertrude thought there was none left within him. His mouth was open. His eyes were open, but fixed on something far away.

And she could not stop her crying.

Gertrude Weiss, eleven years old, knelt down by the wounded man. She bent over his face to see whether he were Dakota or Gypsy or perhaps a neighbor. Closer and closer she leaned, until her black hair came down in billows and her tears rained upon his face, on his cheeks and his eyes. *Ah, see? When the water falls on his eyes, the wounded man begins to blink.*

Then Gertrude noticed that her tears were thickening upon his skin, like a lotion. On impulse she touched it with the tips of her fingers. Yes, as soft as salve were her tears upon him. She began to massage his brow, and straightway the whole winter's night was filled with the fragrance of that ointment.

Gertrude did not cease crying, but a dear gratitude entered into the sound of it now. For the man had opened his eyes, and her chafing was bringing the color back to his flesh again, and the wound in his forehead was healing, and he himself, by his own two hands, was wiping it dry with her hair.

Oh, how sweet was the scent of it all, tears and flesh and hands and hair.

Softly, softly, the man said, "You have done a beautiful thing for me." He parted the hair away from her face and pointed behind her. "Look," he said.

She did. Gertrude turned around and began to grin with the joy of it, for there were all her animals. They had themselves nudged the barn door open and had all trooped forth in a flock of celebration.

"Balthazar," she said to one of her papa's draft horses, and to the other, "Melchior!" She rose up and buried her face in their necks. She felt fur and snaps of static against her ankle, but when she reached down to stroke the cat, the animal shot away. The cat and all her kittens, the horses, the chickens, two collie dogs, one milch cow, four goats, and the entire flock of sheep were forming an adoring audience around the man—who, when Gertrude herself turned to look at him again, was standing tall and robed in glory.

In his face was the very sun for loving. In his eyes were life and strength and a perfect knowledge of the girl before him.

And in his hands was a box, a curiously carven wooden box.

"Gertrude," the man said, his voice as rich as many waters, "this is the evening for giving. The gifts you've given to me, I give them back to you again."

He opened the box, and one by one he set marvelous things upon the white snow:

First, a golden ball. "Gold," he said, "which was given to me as king, and to you as a woman rich with virtue."

Second, a small lamp made cunningly of silver with holes for smoke to escape and three bright chains to swing it by. "Frankincense," he said, "which was given to me as the Son of God, and to you as the girl who prays, whose prayers are pleasant to me."

Third, an alabaster flask filled with ointment. "Myrrh," he said, "which was given to me for my dying, and to you for the sharing of all that I am."

Gertrude stood in the snow, unmoving, her heart burning within her, her face blazing for gladness and mystery.

"Gertrude Weiss," the man said softly. "The next time I come, there shall no one be crying, for I shall come to take you home forever. But for now, go into your own little house and wake your parents with these words. Say to them, *Merry Christmas,* and they shall surely wake rejoicing."

Sing Softly the Cherries

Sing softly the cherries,
   Red, red, sweet and good;
Sing apples and oranges,
   The cinnamon food.

Dance swiftly the cider
   Spin more than you should;
For liquor and laughter
   Will lighten your load.

Declaim the roast turkey
   And riddle the sauce,
Potatoes are stories
   Of riches and loss.

Pipe merrily carrots,
    Drum beets till they bleed;
They root down to darkness
    Who started as seed.

Oh, candy the greetings
    You give to your guests;
The wassail is fleeting
    And life ends in death.

So taffy your handshake
    And ginger the kiss;
Bake huggings like muffins,
    A brave eucharist!

Be feast for our Christmas
    And I'll be the food;
Beg Christ to assist us
    In everything good.

In the Perfect
Center of All
My Circles

A plain photograph of the birth of Jesus would be altogether unremarkable—except that it showed a woman bearing her baby in a public place. That might cause a remark or two. Polite society could find the photo offensive ("Shameless! The homeless have no shame"). Social activists could criticize polite society itself ("Don't blame the victim! Bearing babies in stables is a sign of a mean society").

But no one would call this photo holy.

That which the camera could record of the nativity of Jesus does not inspire awe. It is either too common or too impoverished. A cold, modern scrutiny, a searching of surfaces only, reveals nothing much meaningful here.

Or let me put it another way: If, for us, reality is material merely; if we gaze at the birth with that modern eye that acknowledges nothing of the spirit, sees nothing divine, demands the hard facts only, data, documentation; if truth for us must be empirical to be believed, then we are left with a photograph of small significance: a derelict husband, an immodest mother, a baby cradled in the feed trough of an outdoor shelter for pack animals, a lean-to, likely, built behind a mud-brick house where travelers slept both on the floor within and on the roof without. Simple, rude, dusty, and bare.

Ah, but those for whom this is the only way to gaze at Christmas must themselves live lives bereft of meaning: nothing immaterial, nothing divine, no awe, never a gasp of adoration, never the sense of personal humiliation before glory nor the shock of personal exaltation when Glory chooses also to bow down and to love.

Such people have chosen a shell-existence, hollow at the core. Today, a fruitless rind; tomorrow, quintessential dust.

Our seeing reveals our souls—whether we conceive of one or not.

So how do we see Christmas?

If we do not recognize in the person of this infant an act of almighty God who here initiates forgiveness for a rebellious world; if we do not see in Jesus the Word made baby flesh, nor honor him as the only premise for any genuine Christmas celebration—then we see with that modern eye merely. Stale, flat, unprofitable.

If the "true meaning of Christmas" is for us some vague sentiment of fellowship and charity and little else, then we see with that modern eye merely. Human goodness is a poor alternative to *Immanuel,* the active, personal presence of God among us. Human goodness is unstable. God is not. Moreover, to celebrate human goodness is to celebrate ourselves—and there never was a self that could elevate itself by staring at the self alone. Mirrors are always on the exact plane with the self staring into them, neither higher nor lower.

If the "spirit of the season" is for us a harried getting and spending, an exchange of gifts, we see with that modern eye merely. Instead of the love of God to redeem us from dying (and so to cause in us his ever-living love), we have that halting human love which might redeem a day from loneliness but which itself must, at the end of the day, die.

If we reduce the glory of the Incarnation to craven phrases like "Season's Greetings" (for fear of offending some customer, some boss, some someone who finds no Christ in Christmas and blames us for the looking), then we have offended God by bowing down before those who see with the modern eye merely. Likewise, "Peace!" is rendered an empty wish apart from the Prince of Peace, and "Joy!" is sourceless apart from him who promises joy. For the world can create a fair illusion of joy, but illusions, when they strike experience, leave people worse than before. And this world has never, never, by its own wisdom and strength, compacted even the lesser, passive joy of a lasting peace.

No. I will not see the scene with that empirical, modern eye.

I refuse to accept the narrow sophistications and dead-eyed adulthoods of a "realistic" world. Christmas should not copy us. We should copy Christmas.

Therefore, I choose to stay a child. And my picture of Christmas shall not be undimensioned, neither as flat as a photograph nor as cold as a news report—no, never as cold as my scientist's case study.

Rather, I will paint my picture with baby awe, wide-eyed, primitive, and faithful. More medieval than modern. More matter than material. And I will call it true: For it sees not what is, but what is not seen. It makes the invisible obvious. And this Truth is a living thing—whom to know, and whom to honor, will make us also *children* of that Truth.

My painting is immense. Stand back to look at it. It is composed of seven concentric circles, each one lesser than the last, though intenser for importance—and all surrounding Jesus.

Orbis Primus

The widest circle is the whole world, dark and cold and winterfast. The universe. All creation yearning for this birth and all of it mute until a word is put within its mouth. This word: *In the beginning was the Word, and the Word was with God, and the Word was God.*

That one.

Orbis Secundus

Just inside the first sphere is another, scarcely smaller than the first because it touches that one everywhere and serves the whole of it. The second is a choir of angels, countless as the stars, bright with white light and expectation, gazing inward, full of news—for heaven itself attends this Advent here!

Orbis Tertius

The third circle is trees, great ancient trees, the giants that stand in the shadow outside civilization, northern forest, the jungle that rots every human road, mountain escarpments covered with timber, the cedars of Lebanon—for it is from the simplest growing things that the beams and boards of the Lord's rude birthing room is built. The third circle is poor and dark and huge with groaning. When you hear it, you might call the sound the wind; I tell you, it is the travail of trees long ago made subject unto vanity, who even now await with eager longing the manifestation of the Son of God.

Of these trees is fashioned a stable—order emerging from the wilder world. But the stable lacks all sign of wealth. It offers no comfort of civilized life. For this King shall be lowborn in order to lift the low on high. The abandoned, the rejected, those that sit outside the gates—free and slaves and the poor—shall be delivered from bondage and lifted to the glory and the liberty of the children of God!

Orbis Quartus

Next are animals, herds and flocks afoot, great streams of obedient beasts and the untamed, too, circling through the midnight forest, gazing inward like the angels, yearning to know the fate of their young: For there are ewes here whose lambs have gone inside that stable; there are cows whose calves are representing the whole species; and there is a donkey whose daughter has borne a woman to the very center of the universe, a woman great with child.

For nature makes a harmony at this Nativity. Fur and feather and human flesh, myriad shapes and yet more myriad voices.

Listen! Listen with the ears of your faith and hear in the roaring of all creatures a choral praise and piety, the melody of the turning earth and the music of the spheres: *Blessing and honor,* they sing, *and glory and power be unto him that sitteth upon the throne and unto the Lamb forever and ever!*

And the lesser lambs and the oxen and that singular donkey answer, *Amen.*

Orbis Quintus

The circle in the circle of the singing animals is a gathering of shepherds whom I paint with the faces of children, smiling, shining, breathless, and reverent. You can see their expressions. There is a lantern in this more intimate space, a single flame. Warmth. Fire.

These are the people of every age who, hearing the news, believe it.

Of course they are children! These are those who, believing the goods news, rush to see it for themselves and now have come in from deepest darkness—through the circles of angels and trees and beasts—to behold with their own eyes a Savior, their Savior, their own dear One, their Lord.

Lulay, lulay, they sing together. *By-by-lulee-lulay.*

Some of the shepherds hold hands. Two are giggling. One weeps. She can't help it. It is what she does when she is overcome with joy—she weeps.

And one near the back of the bunch is called Walt.

That's me.

Orbis Sextus

Circle six is a man and a woman. One is standing, one reclined in weariness. The man is Joseph, the adoptive father who lends house and heart and lineage to his precious son. The woman is Mary, the mother, regal and transcendently lovely, for heaven crossed all circles to choose her; and she, when heaven came near nine months ago, said, *Let it be.*

Immediately upon her faithful response it did indeed begin to be.

It happened! And it happens still because it happened that once.

Ah, children! The sixth circle must be the circle composed of time: the year in the middle of all years, the first day of that year. For this woman's riding on one daughter of the donkeys; for her lying down on straw, her straining forward to bear a King, and crying out in dear pain her own verse of the universal hymn; for the crowning of her baby, the infant-skull pressed against the deeps of her most human womanhood—all this is the beginning of meaning in the history of humankind!

For it is this that keeps creation from the annihilations of absurdity—this: that on a particular day, in a particular place, within the womb of a particular woman, the fullness of God was pleased to rise through human flesh to be born as flesh himself into the world.

It happened! *She brought forth her firstborn son, and wrapped him in swaddling clothes, and—*

Orbis Septimus

—and the smallest circle of the seven, meaner than the others, is that manger of wood.

Wood, lumber from the forests: For Jesus was born material truly, bone and flesh and a red-running blood.

But wood, rough planks hewn by human hands: For one day wood would kill him.

Wood is the bracket of the earthly existence of the Lord Jesus Christ. Wood is the smallest compass around him, for it is our sinning and his loving—which, taken together, shape the very person of the Christ. This is his personal form both visible and invisible, a servant, a body obedient unto death, even death on a cross.

For here, in a sphere which is the size of any human being, is the Truth which cannot be seen but which my painting depicts in an outrageous round of wood as in a carving: that his life, enclosed by a cradle and a cross, saves ours thereby.

Oh, my dear, you are in the picture too! Do you see yourself? Kneeling next to Wally? And in our hands, hammers.

In his tiny baby hands, two nails.

Centrum Orbium Omnium

But then here, in the perfect center of all my circles and of all the spheres of all the world; here, in the center of the galaxies; in the center of thought and love and human gesture, blazing with light more lovely than sunlight, a light that makes of Mary a madonna, light that can kindle wood to burn a sacred flame, light that cancels in fire our hammers and that shows on your brow even now a crown of life, light that lightens the Gentiles and the dark pathways of all creatures and forests—

—here, I say, in the center of everything, brightening all things even to the extremes of time and eternity—

—here, himself the center that holds all orbits in one grand and universal dance—

—is Jesus.

Here! Come and see! Can you see the tiny baby born? Can you see the Infant King? And can you recognize in him *Immanuel?*

Amen, child! O wide-eyed child all filled with awe, amen: For now you are seeing Christmas.

Mary's Carol

And Mary said, He remembered me,
He remembered his maiden of low degree:
With tender care and gentility
    He remembered me.

I breathe, and my breathing laughs in the Lord;
I live, and my life enlarges his name,
For I have heard
His mighty word,
Obeyed his bright, genetic word,
And I that Word contain.

    And Mary said, He remembers me.
    In my silence and my singularity
    He lifts his maid from her low degree:
        He remembers me.

But all of the women, all of the men,
All of the children fearing his name—
He mercies them,
God mercies them,
Reveals his strong right arm to them,
And sweeps the proud away.

And Mary said, He remembers you;
He will lead you, exalt you, and love you, too.
Children of old, O be children new!
He remembers you.

And who are the full? God gives them no food.
And where are the hungry? He fills them with good!
The powerful
By God shall fall;
The rich remember how to crawl,
The poor rise up renewed.

And Mary said, He remembers well
All he promised to give unto Israel,
When Abraham in the stars beheld
His descendants here!

And Mary said, He remembers me;
He has made me the place of the Savior-seed,
O Lord, let it be that I like you
    Will remember you,

    Will remember you—
Too.

The Carol of the Seven Signs

WORDS BY WALT WANGERIN, JR.   MUSIC BY DENNIS FRIESEN-CARPER

For the Valparaiso University Kantorei
Dr. Lorraine Brugh, conductor
Advent/Christmas Vespers, 1999

Sing Softly the Cherries

WORDS BY WALT WANGERIN, JR.   MUSIC BY KEN MEDEMA

Contact Brier Patch Music to order the choral version of this chorus. Call 888-KEN-KEN-KEN

beets till they bleed; They root down to dark - ness Who

start———————ed as seed.——————— Oh,

can - dy the—— greet - ings You give to your guests;———

_ The was - sail is—— fleet - ing And life ends in

death.——————— So taf - fy— your— hand - shake And

gin - ger the kiss; Bake hug - gings like muf - fins, A

brave——————— eu - cha - rist!——————— Be

feast— for— our— Christ - mas And I'll be the food; Beg

Christ to as - sist us In ev'———————

———ry - thing good.———————

Mary's Carol

WORDS BY WALT WANGERIN, JR.   MUSIC BY RANDY COURTS

And Ma-ry said, He re - mem-bered me, He re - mem-bered his maid - en of

low de-gree:___ With ten-der care and gen - ti - li-ty He re - mem - bered

me.___ I breathe, and my breath - ing laughs in the Lord;___ I

live, and my life___ en - larg-es his name,___ For I have heard His might-y word, O-

beyed his bright, ge - net - ic word, And I that Word con - tain.___ And

Ma - ry said, He re - mem-bers me. In my si - lence and my___ sin - gu -

lar - i - ty___ He lifts his maid from her low de-gree: He re - mem - bers

me. But all of the wo - men, all of the men,—

All of the child - ren fear-ing his name— He mer-cies them, God mer-cies them, Re-

veals his strong right arm to them, And sweeps the proud a-way.— And

Ma - ry said, He re - mem-bers you; He will lead you, ex - alt— you, and

love you, too.— Child - ren of old, O be child - ren new! He re-

mem - bers you.— And

who are the full?— God gives them no food.— And where are the hun - gry? He

fills them with good!— The pow - er - ful By God shall fall; The

rich re-mem-ber how to crawl, The poor rise up re-newed._____ And

Ma-ry said, He re-mem-bers well All he pro-mised to give____ un-to

Is-ra-el, When A-bra-ham in the stars be-held His de-scen-dants

here!_____ And

Ma-ry said, He re-mem-bers me; He has made me the place____ of the

Sav-ior-seed, O Lord, let it be____ that I like you Will re-

mem-ber you,_____ Will re-

mem-ber you—____ Too._____

164